W9-APX-919

A Peculiar Institution:
Slavery in the Plantation South

Lucent Library of Black History

Stephen Currie

LUCENT BOOKS

An imprint of Thomson Gale, a part of The Thomson Corporation

THOMSON

™

GALE

Detroit • New York • San Francisco • San Diego • New Haven, Conn.
Waterville, Maine • London • Munich

THOMSON

━━━✦━━━ ™

GALE

© 2005 Thomson Gale, a part of The Thomson Corporation.

Thomson and Star Logo are trademarks and Gale and Lucent Books are registered trademarks used herein under license.

For more information, contact
Lucent Books
27500 Drake Rd.
Farmington Hills, MI 48331-3535
Or you can visit our Internet site at http://www.gale.com

ALL RIGHTS RESERVED.
No part of this work covered by the copyright hereon may be reproduced or used in any form or by any means—graphic, electronic, or mechanical, including photocopying, recording, taping, Web distribution or information storage retrieval systems—without the written permission of the publisher.

Every effort has been made to trace the owners of copyrighted material.

LIBRARY OF CONGRESS CATALOGING-IN-PUBLICATION DATA

Currie, Stephen, 1960–
    Slavery in the plantation South / by Stephen Currie.
        p. cm. — (Lucent library of Black history)
Includes bibliographical references and index.
ISBN 1-59018-704-0 (alk. paper)
1. Slavery—Southern States—History—Juvenile literature. 2. Slaves—Southern States—Social conditions—Juvenile literature. 3. Plantation life—Southern States—History—Juvenile literature. 4. Southern States—Social life and customs—1775–1865—Juvenile literature. 5. Southern States—Race relations—Juvenile literature. 6. Southern States—Social conditions—Juvenile literature. I. Title. II. Series.
E441.C87 2005
306.3'62'0975—dc22
                                                                    2004030304

Printed in the United States of America

Contents

Foreword

It has been more than 500 years since Africans were first brought to the New World in shackles, and over 140 years since slavery was formally abolished in the United States. Over fifty years have passed since the fallacy of "separate but equal" was obliterated in the American courts, and some 40 years since the watershed Civil Rights Act of 1965 guaranteed the rights and liberties of all Americans, especially those of color. Over time, these changes have become celebrated landmarks in American history. In the twenty-first century, African-American men and women are politicians, judges, diplomats, professors, deans, doctors, artists, athletes, business owners, and home owners. For many, the scars of the past have melted away in the opportunities that have been found in contemporary society. Observers such as Peter N. Kirsanow, who sits on the U.S. Commission of Civil Rights, point to these accomplishments and conclude, "The growing black middle class may be viewed as proof that most of the civil rights battles have been won."

In spite of these legal victories, however, prejudice and inequality have persisted in American society. In 2003, African-Americans comprised just 12 percent of the nation's population, yet accounted for 44 percent of its prison inmates and 24 percent of its poor. Racially motivated hate crimes continue to appear on the pages of major newspapers in many American cities. Furthermore, many African-Americans still experience either overt or muted racism in their daily lives. A 1996 study undertaken by Professor Nancy Krieger of the Harvard School of Public Health, for example, found that 80 percent of the African-American participants reported having experienced racial discrimination in one or more settings, including at work or school, applying for housing and medical care, from the police or in the courts, and on the street or in a public setting.

It is for these reasons that many believe the struggle for racial equality and justice is far from over. These episodes of discrimination threaten to shatter the illusion that America has completely overcome its racist past, causing many black Americans to become increasingly frustrated and confused. Scholar and writer Ellis Cose has described this splintered state in the following way: "'I have done everything I was supposed to do. I have stayed out of trouble with the law, gone to the right schools, and worked myself nearly to death. What more do they want? Why in God's name won't they accept me as a full human being?" For Cose and others, the struggle for equality and justice has yet to be fully achieved.

In many subtle yet important ways, the traumatic experiences of slavery and segregation continue to inform the way race is discussed and experienced in the twenty-first century. Indeed, it is possible that America will always grapple with the fallout from its distressing past. Ulric Haynes, dean of the Hofstra University School of Business has said, "Perhaps race will always matter, given the historical circumstances under which we came to this country." But studying this past and understanding how it contributes to present-day dialogues about race and history in America is a critical component of contemporary education. To this end, the Lucent Library of Black History offers a thorough look at the experiences that have shaped the black community and the American people as a whole. Annotated bibliographies provide readers with ideas for further research, while fully documented primary and secondary source quotations enhance the text. Each book in the series explores a different episode of black history; together they provide students with a wealth of information as well as launching points for further study and discussion.

The Peculiar Institution

Few institutions have played as tragic, as divisive, or as distinctive a role in American history as slavery. Few have had such an enormous impact on individual Americans, both black and white, and the nation as a whole. American slavery helped shape a culture and an economy. It forced millions of Americans to suffer in a system both brutal and unfair. And in the end, slavery came very near to destroying the United States itself.

But in the early 1600s, when the first Africans arrived on the eastern coast of North America, no one could have predicted that slavery would become such a potent force. The institution was slow to find a foothold. Even once it became accepted, slavery's early development was slow, haphazard, and inconsistent from one place to the next. Few early colonists were slaveholders, and even fewer were slaves. As a result, slavery was only a minor part of the early economic and political landscape of what would become the United States.

That would change dramatically. For a variety of political, economic, and technological reasons, the enslavement of Africans became more common, more organized, and even more firmly entrenched. The slave population, tiny at first, sharply increased. In 1750, about a century after white Americans first began to enslave blacks, fewer than 250,000 slaves lived in Britain's North American colonies. Just a hundred years later, the number of slaves stood at nearly 4 million. Once, slavery had been in the background of American life. By the middle of the nineteenth century, it increasingly took center stage.

American Slavery

What slavery meant was simple enough. American slaves were property, forced to work without pay whenever and however their masters pleased. According to the law, slaves were not fully human, and therefore not worthy of protection from any but the most inhumane acts. While some masters were kind, generous, and tolerant toward their slaves, many others were not. Slaves suffered from beatings and overwork, and were denied appropriate food, housing, and medical care. Many were sold away from their own children, parents, or spouses. Slavery, in short, was a system under which slaves had few rights that any white person was bound to respect.

In these regards, slavery was far from unique to the United States. On the contrary, slavery had a long and complex history across the globe. It had been practiced by cultures ranging from the ancient Greeks and the Hebrews of the Old Testament to the Aztecs of Mexico and the West Africans of the nineteenth century. But the form of slavery that appeared in the United States differed from that practiced in many other places and times. Most notably, American slavery was both racial and hereditary. It was racial because, by law, only blacks could be enslaved. And it was hereditary because a slave's descendants were destined to be enslaved as well. Together, these two features gave American slavery its distinctive character.

By the nineteenth century, slavery had reached the pinnacle of its American development. It had also become regionally confined. No longer was slavery a generically American institution. Instead, it had become concentrated exclusively in the agricultural southern half of the country. This area, sometimes referred to by historians as the plantation South, extended from the states of Florida and Texas as far north as Maryland, Kentucky, and Missouri. North of that line, slavery did not survive long into the nineteenth century. South of it, however, the institution

TO BE SOLD, on board the Ship *Bance-Island*, on tuesday the 6th of *May* next, at *Ashley-Ferry*; a choice cargo of about 250 fine healthy NEGROES, just arrived from the Windward & Rice Coast. —The utmost care has already been taken, and shall be continued, to keep them free from the least danger of being infected with the SMALL-POX, no boat having been on board, and all other communication with people from *Charles-Town* prevented.

Austin, Laurens, & Appleby.

N. B. Full one Half of the above Negroes have had the SMALL-POX in their own Country.

A poster guarantees the health of the slaves to be sold at an upcoming auction. By the mid-nineteenth century, the slave population in the United States totaled nearly 4 million.

not only persisted but flourished. White southerners, using the word *peculiar* in the sense of "distinctive," spoke with pride of their "peculiar institution" of slavery.

A National Impact

Still, just because slavery had become associated with only one geographic region did not mean its impact stopped at the borders of the South. The rising importance of slavery to the southern states began to influence everything from southern opinions on the acquisition of new territory to northerners' ideas of decency and justice. By the middle of the nineteenth century, slavery was at the heart of most political, moral, and economic discussions throughout the United States.

Directly and indirectly, the question of slavery sparked dozens of controversies and arguments, some minor but others of great national importance. Partisans on both sides argued the ethics of slavery, the brutality of the institution, and the legality of requiring northerners to send runaway slaves back to their owners. Southerners staunchly defended their institution from an increasing barrage of northern attacks and accused northern antislavery activists of hypocrisy for condemning slavery while profiting from the manufacture and sale of southern cotton.

By the middle of the nineteenth century, the debate over slavery had created an enormous rift between South and North. Though once it had been possible to bridge this rift through negotiation and compromise, it was becoming increasingly clear that such political solutions were stopgaps. As President Abraham Lincoln warned, the United States would have to accept or reject slavery entirely or be destroyed. In the end it would take a violent and destructive war to resolve the question of American slavery for good.

Chapter One

The Beginnings of Slavery

The first European colonists in North America did not practice slavery. In 1607, when the earliest permanent English settlement was established at Jamestown, Virginia, every colonist was both white and free. Together, these new settlers built houses, cleared land for farms, and labored to plant and harvest their crops, the most notable of which was tobacco, a New World plant that fetched high prices in Europe. Thanks to the profits from tobacco, the colony seemed to have a bright future. The only problem was an acute shortage of labor. There were simply not enough workers to produce all the tobacco colonial leaders could sell.

Early on, the Virginia colonists tried to remedy the situation by enslaving local natives. The settlers did manage to capture a number of Indians, who were then put to work tending the valuable tobacco crop. But the Indians knew the area well, and they had friends and family nearby. Short of keeping their native captives constantly in chains, the colonists could not prevent the Indian laborers from disappearing into the forests. Moreover, since the first English settlers relied partly on the goodwill of the Indians for survival, enslaving them was not only counterproductive but foolish. As a result, colonial leaders soon abandoned the idea of forcing the Native Americans into slavery.

Instead, the colonists turned to England for the workers they needed. They spread the word that Virginia was a very wealthy land where anyone could easily make a fortune. Eager to share in the riches, England's poor soon began flocking to Jamestown. Because most of these men and women could not afford the voyage, settlers already in the colony paid for their passage. In

In this woodcut, Virginia colonists unload a captive Native American man from a boat. As their slave, the Indian will be forced to toil in their tobacco fields.

exchange, the new arrivals agreed to work for their sponsors for five to seven years, a period of time known as an indenture. The people who agreed to be bound in this way were known as indentured servants.

Most indentured servants, however, soon realized that getting rich once they were through with their indentures was by no means guaranteed. Moreover, the life of an indentured servant was hardly a life of ease. The new settlers endured heavy workloads and long workdays. Though some masters treated their ser-

In this twentieth-century painting, armed colonists stand guard over the first Africans brought to Jamestown in 1619.

vants with gentleness and respect, most did not. Physical punishment was commonplace, and servants had few rights until their contracts of indenture expired.

Word soon began to spread throughout England that conditions in Virginia were not as promised. As a result, the number of indentured servants arriving from England began to decline by the 1630s. At the same time, however, Virginia's need for more laborers continued to grow. Clearly, another source of labor would have to be found.

The First African Americans

The answer arrived almost by accident. In August 1619 a Dutch trading ship put in at the Jamestown harbor. The ship's passengers included a group of Africans who had been taken by the Dutch in a battle with a Spanish vessel. Today, no one knows the names of the African captives or the name of the ship that brought them to Virginia. But the events of the day are not in doubt. The Dutch captain, wrote colonist John Rolfe, "sold us twenty Negars [Negroes]."[1]

These "twenty Negars" were the first Africans to arrive in the English colonies. The leaders of the young colony, seeing an opportunity, immediately put the Africans to work. Though clear records are lacking, the Africans evidently acquitted themselves well. Most likely, they proved to be good laborers: strong, able, and quite possibly immune to some of the common Virginia diseases, such as malaria and yellow fever, that often sickened and killed the Europeans. In any case, colonial leaders soon sought out more African laborers. Over the next few decades, a steady procession of Africans arrived in Jamestown.

These Africans did not travel to Virginia by choice. They were taken forcibly by sea captains who hoped to sell them to the colonists, just as the anonymous Dutch captain had done in 1619. Still, these first African Americans were not slaves as the term would be understood today. Their status was largely indistinguishable from that of Virginia's white indentured servants. Although the terms of indenture were sometimes longer for the blacks and their treatment more severe, there was no sense that their servitude would last forever. In fact, plenty of Africans in early Virginia were given their freedom after completing their time of service. "Now I know myne owne ground," remarked one of these newly free men, "and I will worke when I please and play when I please."[2]

From Servant to Slave

But within a few years, the status of blacks in Virginia—and elsewhere in the British colonies—began to deteriorate. By 1650 it was common for blacks, unlike whites, to have terms of indenture that encompassed their entire lifetimes, and sometimes beyond. In 1652, for instance, a white Virginian purchased a ten-year-old black girl named Jowan. The transaction specified that Jowan's new master would have the right to Jowan's labor for the remainder of her life. It also specified that the master and his heirs were entitled to the labor of "her Issue and produce [that is, her children] . . . for their Life tyme. And their Successors forever."[3]

Before long, cases like Jowan's were the norm, not the exception. For Africans, indentured servitude no longer existed. In 1660 the Virginia legal system formally acknowledged that for blacks in Virginia, slavery applied not just to the slave but to his or her descendants. Other British colonies, such as Maryland and South Carolina, soon imitated Virginia. Even northern colonies such as Massachusetts incorporated slavery into their laws. By the 1670s, the idea of racial, hereditary African slavery had taken hold across the British colonies. For Americans of African descent, enslavement would now be perpetual.

Gradually, the prospects of blacks in the New World dimmed. New laws reflected the idea that slaves were property. South Carolina's leaders recognized that masters had "absolute power and authority"[4] over their black slaves. The message was clear: Africans in America had no rights, and were entitled to none.

Slavery and Race

The rise of slavery in the American colonies was not simply about filling a labor shortage. If obtaining more workers had been the only reason for slavery, then *all* indentured servants might have been enslaved by the wealthiest colonists. But white servants escaped this fate; permanent bondage was reserved for blacks alone. The reasons for this distinction lie in European attitudes about race.

"The Casual Killing of Slaves"

In 1669 Virginia passed a law concerning "the casual killing of slaves" by their masters. The following excerpt from the law, quoted in Donald R. Wright's *African Americans in the Colonial Era*, gives slaves a far lower status than that of the indentured blacks who arrived fifty years earlier:

> Be it enacted and declared by this grand assembly, if any slave resist his master[,] (or other by his masters order correcting him) and by the extremity of the correction should chance to die, that his death shall not be accompted [considered] Felony, but the master (or that other person appointed by the master to punish him) be acquit[ted] from molestation, since it cannot be presumed that prepensed malice [that is, the intention to cause harm] . . . should induce any man to destroy his own estate [property].

In effect, the law argued that since slaves were property, the slaveholder who killed a slave was harming only himself. A farmer who destroyed his own plow in an attempt to repair it would not be jailed or fined; indeed, the state would consider the incident none of its business. By similar reasoning, the death of a slave was no one's business but the farmer's.

A crowd of colonists in New York watches as a disobedient slave is burned at the stake in public.

Significant European contact with the dark-skinned people of West Africa had begun in the 1400s, when explorers from Portugal and other nations had sailed along the African coastline. Throughout this period of contact, most Europeans looked down on blacks as inferior. The citizens of Europe believed that they lived in the most advanced society on the globe. By comparison, Europeans agreed, the cultures of Africa seemed hopelessly backward and ignorant. The Africans' technology was seen as inferior, their customs barbaric, their religions mere superstition. Even their manners and hygiene marked them as uncivilized. "They are a hideous people," one English writer charged, "and stink exceedingly."[5]

Europeans, therefore, saw nothing wrong in enslaving a people they viewed as uncivilized. But the British colonists in North America, like their counterparts in Europe, had an even more powerful rationale for black slavery: their religion. The Bible, they pointed out, not only accepted slavery but justified it. According to the Old Testament book of Leviticus, for example, "Both thy bondmen, and thy bondmaids, which thou shalt have," read Leviticus 25:44, "shall be of the heathen that are round about you." To the early North American colonists, "heathen" meant non-Christian, and Africans certainly qualified.

Slaveholders likewise agreed that the Bible approved of slavery in perpetuity. "Ye shall take [slaves] as an inheritance for your children after you," read Leviticus 25:46; "they shall be your bondmen for ever." The New Testament did not contradict this view. Nowhere in the Gospels was Jesus portrayed as denouncing slavery. Neither did the apostle Paul, an instrumental figure in shaping Christian thought. On the contrary, slaveholders pointed out, one of Paul's works instructed slaves to remain obedient at all times.

The European religious tradition also provided a reason why the enslavement of Africans in particular made sense. Part of the biblical story of the Great Flood held that Noah had been deeply offended at one point by his son Ham. According to the book of Genesis, Noah had exacted revenge by dooming Ham's son Canaan to perpetual servitude. Although the Bible never said so directly, most European Christians believed that the people of Africa were Canaan's descendants. If so—and most colonists had no reason to doubt it—then the Bible clearly justified the enslavement of blacks.

"Nine Bars and Two Brass Rings"

The experiences of their neighbors also pushed the English colonists to accept slavery. Long before slavery arrived in British North America, the institution had already been introduced elsewhere in the New World—most notably by the Portuguese in Brazil and by a variety of colonial powers in the Caribbean. By 1540, a century before slavery became common in Virginia, traders were bringing thousands of West Africans each year to these parts of the Americas. These slaves were part of what became known as the Atlantic slave trade, which would eventually be expanded to include the North American colonies as well.

In its broad outlines, the slave trade was simple enough. European captains began the process by visiting ports along the coast of West Africa. There a captain might send out a raiding party to capture natives and bring them aboard the vessel. More often, however, the Europeans bargained with West African tribal leaders or their representatives to buy the slaves they sought.

Sadly, there was no shortage of potential captives. The tribes of the region had a long history of taking slaves, particularly during warfare. The most powerful leaders in the area thus had plenty of captives to sell or to trade. Prices varied from port to port and from one year to the next; units of currency did too. One king, for instance, announced that he would sell slaves at the fixed rate of "thirteen [iron] bars for males, and nine bars and two brass rings for females."[6] Other leaders sought guns, tobacco, or cowrie shells, a currency that was accepted all along the West African coast.

Whatever the details of the exchanges, the slave trade enriched not only the Europeans but the West African leaders as well. By sending war prisoners to another continent, tribal leaders increased their wealth, depopulated their enemies, and consolidated their power. For the most part, West African leaders did not see any drawbacks in the burgeoning transatlantic slave trade. African leaders viewed the world in tribal, rather than racial, terms. They felt no solidarity with other Africans just on the basis of skin color. The white traders simply represented a new market for an established product. In the minds of the monarchs, there

was no distinction between selling a captive to a neighboring community and selling one to a white trader to bring to the New World.

Across the Atlantic

But to the captive, of course, there was literally a world of difference. Those who stayed in West Africa still recognized the languages, the geography, and the natural features around them. Going to the New World, in contrast, meant adjusting to new lands, peoples, and ways of life. "Their complexions [differed] so much from ours," remembered Virginia slave Olaudah Equiano about the Europeans who purchased him. "The language they spoke . . . was very different from any I had ever heard."[7]

Ease of adjustment was not the only difference between slavery in Africa and slavery in the New World. Whether through escape, ransom, or recapture, for instance, slaves who stayed near their West African homes had a chance of returning to their families. Those taken to the New World, however, had no such hope. Nor was West African slavery as permanent as its American counterpart. West African slaves could sometimes purchase their free-

Captive Africans bound in chains and yokes make the long journey to the coast to board ships bound for the Americas.

dom or otherwise become accepted as full members of their new societies, and their children and grandchildren had an even better chance of doing so. Moving out of slavery was possible in the New World as well, but it was much less common—and typically much more difficult.

Perhaps the main difference between slaves bound for the New World and those who remained in Africa, though, was not the destination—but the journey. Depending on the ship and the prevailing winds, it could take several weeks to travel from the West African coast to the New World. Under the best of circumstances, this voyage was miserable. Even the crews of these slave-carrying vessels complained bitterly about the endless waves, the cramped quarters, and the lack of fresh food.

For the slaves, the voyage—sometimes known as the Middle Passage—was far worse. Though a handful of captains attempted to be kind toward their African prisoners, the vast majority made no such effort. They beat their captives for infractions real and imagined, made no effort to treat or prevent disease, and offered

Slave traders packed Africans into cramped, airless cargo holds below their ships' decks (top) and brutalized the prisoners (bottom) during the long voyage across the Atlantic.

only minimal amounts and varieties of food. "The diet of the negroes, while on board," noted ship's doctor Alexander Falconbridge in 1788, "consists chiefly of horsebeans, boiled to the consistence of a pulp; of boiled yams and rice, and sometimes of a small quantity of beef or pork."[8]

Tight Spaces and Chains

The indignities of poor diet and regular beatings, however, were easy to bear compared to the worst horror of the slave ships: an almost complete lack of space and fresh air. Most captives were confined in small, low spaces below the main decks of their ships. These spaces were generally designed to hold barrels and other cargo; they had not been built with humans in mind. "There was hardly standing, lying, or sitting room," observes historian John Hope Franklin. "Chained together by twos, hands and feet, slaves had no room in which to move about and no freedom to exercise their bodies even in the slightest."[9]

Because every slave represented potential profit, it was in the captain's interest to squeeze as many people as possible into these compartments. Many ships carried more than four hundred slaves on a single voyage, which usually meant jamming human beings into spaces no more than one foot wide. Some captains loaded as many as six hundred prisoners onto a single ship. With fewer prisoners, crew members could sometimes bring the slaves above deck for exercise and fresh air. On seriously overcrowded voyages, however, the slaves never stirred from their shipboard prisons.

Such conditions belowdecks frequently allowed disease to spread. Viruses and bacteria jumped quickly from one host to another, usually with devastating consequences. On Falconbridge's ship, for instance, an illness similar to dysentery broke out among the slaves during the voyage. "The deck was so covered with blood and mucus which had proceeded from [the slaves]," noted Falconbridge, "that it resembled a slaughterhouse."[10]

Not surprisingly, death rates on the slave ships were horrendous. On some ships, more than half the captives died before reaching the Americas. Disease and starvation were the most common killers. But because of the appalling conditions, some slaves chose to end their lives by refusing to eat or—if they could seize the opportunity—by throwing themselves overboard. Those who survived sometimes wished they had done the same. "Often did I think many of the inhabitants of the deep [that is, the slaves who had jumped overboard] more happy than myself," remembered Olaudah Equiano. "I envied them the freedom they enjoyed."[11]

The Slave Market

The end of the Middle Passage was not the end of captives' misery. Each ship had a particular destination: a port along the North and South American coastline or in the Caribbean. As soon as the ships arrived at these ports, workers hurried the surviving slaves down the gangplanks and caged them in pens. These were the slave markets of the New World. Here the African prisoners would stay, fearful and exhausted, until they were sold to the highest bidder.

The workings of these sales varied from port to port and from one decade to another. Sometimes entrepreneurs held formal auctions. Sometimes they simply announced the arrival of new prisoners and negotiated prices with prospective purchasers. Either way, the process was dehumanizing and grim. Farmers, tradespeople, and investors poked and prodded the captives, looking for a bargain. Strength, endurance, age, health, the potential for producing children—all helped determine how much a buyer might pay.

Through the 1600s and into the 1700s, few slave ships traveled directly to British North America. The demand for labor—and, accordingly, the offering price for African slaves—was much higher on islands such as Cuba and Hispaniola (the land divided in modern times between the nations of Haiti and the Dominican Republic). Thus, it made no sense for entrepreneurs and ship captains to bring slaves to Jamestown, Charleston, or New York when Caribbean destinations promised a much greater reward. Consequently, early American slave traders bought slaves at Caribbean markets and then transported their purchases north for resale.

But as the British colonies grew, and as slavery became more important to their economies, prices fetched by slaves in British North America began to rise. Before long, a procession of ships was sailing from West Africa directly to slave markets in the colonies. From these ports, slaves were dispersed to farms, towns, and villages. "To be sold, by John Lyon," read a typical colonial advertisement, "twenty-three fine healthy young slaves, just arrived from the Coast of Africa."[12]

"Unalienable Rights" and Slavery

During the American Revolution, for the first time, many colonists began to see a problem with slavery. The reason was the contradiction between slavery and the rhetoric of revolutionary leaders. The colonists couched many of their arguments for independence in terms of human rights and natural laws. Nowhere was this sentiment expressed more clearly or more enthusiastically than in the preamble to the Declaration of Independence. "We hold these truths to be self-evident," reads one of the most famous lines in this document, "that all men are created equal, that they are endowed by their Creator with certain unalienable rights, that among these are Life, Liberty, and the pursuit of Happiness."

Some white colonists soon recognized that phrases such as "unalienable rights" and "created equal" could be applied not just to their own position but to the circumstances of American slaves as well. The realization unsettled many Americans and made them question the institution they had taken for granted.

Blacks, too, noted the discrepancy between the colonists' words and deeds. In 1773 four Massachusetts slaves petitioned the colonial legislature for their freedom. Their argument began with the statement (quoted in Kelley and Lewis's *To Make Our World Anew*), "We expect great things from men who have made such a noble stand against the designs of their fellow-man to enslave them." The following year, another group of Massachusetts slaves reminded the colonial governor that all Americans had a right to freedom. The idea of liberty was in the air. And while revolution raged, both blacks and whites found it hard to justify demanding it for some and denying it to others.

African Prisoners

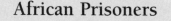

John (or Jean) Barbot was a French explorer and official who spent some time in West Africa during the 1600s. His writings include a detailed description of the transatlantic slave trade and its workings. In this excerpt from his works, quoted in Basil Davidson's *The African Slave Trade*, Barbot explains the degrading process by which the slaves were sold to European traders and prepared for shipment to the New World.

> As the slaves come down to Fida [a coastal town] from the inland country, they are put into a booth or prison, built for that purpose, near the beach, all of them together; and when the Europeans are to receive them, they are brought out into a large plain, where the [ships'] surgeons examine every part of every one of them . . . men and women being all stark naked. Such as are allowed [determined to be] good and sound, are set on one side, and the others by themselves; which slaves so rejected are called Mackrons, being above 35 years of age, or defective in their lips, eyes, or teeth, or grown grey; or that have the venereal disease, or any other imperfection. . . . Each of the others, which have passed as good, is marked on the breast with a red-hot iron, imprinting the mark of the French, English or Dutch companies, that so each nation may distinguish their own. . . . In this particular, care is taken that the women, as tenderest, be not burnt too hard. The branded slaves, after this, are returned to their former booths [to await shipment].

An American Institution

The increase in the number of slave ships sailing to North America had a predictable effect on the slave population of the colonies. In 1700 there were an estimated 28,000 slaves spread across the thirteen colonies. A quarter century later, that figure had nearly tripled. And by 1750 the number of slaves stood at about 236,000. In just fifty years, the colonial slave population had increased nearly tenfold. Births among slaves accounted for some of the rapid population growth. Most of the increase, however, was the result of importation from Africa.

As the number of slaves rose, the way that white Americans thought about slavery began to change. Before 1700, slavery simply had not affected the lives of most colonists. Few European Americans owned slaves; many did not know a single slaveholding family. If slavery had disappeared—if all slaves had been set free and no further African captives had been imported into the colonies—most Americans would have paid little attention.

By 1750, however, that was no longer true. Slavery had expanded in both scope and influence. Particularly in the southern colonies, where most of the slaves lived, the institution had become a normal and unremarkable part of society. Slaves worked the fields, producing not only tobacco but also cotton, rice, and sugar. They labored as maids and butlers, cooked and cleaned, and made goods ranging from shoes to metal. As the colonies grew, slavery grew too, an important factor in the flourishing colonial economy. Well before the founding of the United States, slavery had become an established American phenomenon.

Chapter Two

The Rise of the Plantation South

Although the American slave population continued to rise sharply as the 1700s progressed, the institution of slavery was still not thoroughly secure. During and immediately after the American Revolution (1775–1783), in fact, slavery reached a cross-roads. For the first time, the economic and moral underpinnings of American slavery were being challenged—in part by people who did not own slaves, but also by many who did. Slavery had become an American institution, but as the 1700s came to an end, it was unclear what path the institution would take. For that matter, it was not obvious that slavery would survive at all.

In the end, slavery went in two separate directions. In the northern states, it died a gradual death. But in the southern states, slavery became vital to prosperity. In the process, slavery changed and grew, and even southerners who did not own slaves came to see the institution as a part of their regional identity. A new phase had begun in the history of slavery: the rise of the plantation South.

Doubt and Debate

Early opposition to slavery in North America had been almost unknown. The first printed antislavery tracts did not appear until the end of the seventeenth century, approximately fifty years after slavery had won legal recognition in most American colonies. Even then, the first tracts attracted little attention and changed few Americans' minds. Most colonists considered slavery justified and appropriate. After all, no less an authority than the Bible had said so.

The authors of the first antislavery pamphlets acknowledged the passages in the Bible that seemed to indicate God's approval of slavery. But they pointed to other passages that, they argued, told a different story. In 1693, for instance, Quaker pamphleteer George Keith pointed to Deuteronomy 24:14, which reads: "Thou shalt not oppress an hired servant that is poor and needy, whether he be of thy brethren, or of the strangers that are in thy land." To Keith, the implications of this verse were clear. "What greater Oppression can there be inflicted upon our Felow Creatures," he wrote, "than is inflicted on the poor Negroes!"[13]

The declaration issued by an anti-slavery convention held in Philadelphia in 1833 includes an illustration of Hercules (a symbol of justice) strangling a lion (the institution of slavery).

In their attacks on slavery, these early writers also appealed to more abstract, less strictly religious ideas of justice and ethics. According to the antislavery activists of the time, Africans were deserving of fair and humane treatment simply by virtue of being human beings. Blacks, these writers conceded, may well have been ignorant, uncivilized, and violent, but they still had the right to be free. "It's shocking to human Nature," wrote a group of antislavery Georgia citizens in 1739, "that any Race of Mankind, and their Posterity, should be sentenced to perpetual Slavery."[14] In this view, slavery violated a fundamental principle of justice.

Regions and Economics

The views of these Georgia residents notwithstanding, doubts about slavery were more commonly expressed in the North than in the South. Disparities in the growth of slavery reflected this difference. The slave population had grown much more rapidly south of the Pennsylvania-Maryland border than north of it. By 1760 only about one slave in every eight lived north of this boundary, and that proportion was dropping steadily.

Part of the reason involved moral concerns. The religious groups most opposed to slavery—notably the Quakers—happened to be more numerous in the northern colonies than in the South. The larger reason, however, was economic. Although masters did not pay slaves for their labor, they did have to pay to feed, clothe, and house them. And buying a slave was expensive. As historian John Hope Franklin puts it, "Slaves were among the most valuable possessions of English people in the New World."[15] As long as slaves performed enough labor, these expenses could be justified. But inactivity forced by the long northern winters meant that slaves were often a drain on their owners' resources. Gradually, northerners concluded that slavery simply did not pay. Instead of buying slaves, they hired free laborers and paid them wages for the hours they actually spent working.

Due to the combination of economics and moral considerations, slavery soon began to disappear in the North. In 1780 Pennsylvania adopted a plan called gradual emancipation. Under this plan, all slaves were promised their freedom within a set period of time. Other northern states freed their slaves as well, either gradually or immediately. By 1790 the elimination of slavery in the North was well under way. Slavery had become a distinctly regional phenomenon, limited to the states south of the Maryland-Pennsylvania border, or, as it would soon be called, the Mason-Dixon Line.

Southern Doubts About Slavery

Even in the South, however, slavery's future was not assured. Many influential southerners, both during and after the Revolution, expressed doubts about the institution. Few of these men went so far as to free all their slaves; in the South, slaves represented a large share of a slaveholder's wealth, so to give slaves their freedom meant accepting a drastically reduced standard of living. Still, many white southerners hoped that someday they might have the ability to free their slaves without suffering a crippling economic loss. Many couched these sentiments in moral terms, much as their counterparts in the North did. "An evil exists which requires a remedy," wrote George Washington. "I wish I could liberate a certain species of property [that is, slaves] which I possess, very repugnantly to my own feelings."[16]

At the same time, some southerners were also beginning to question the economic value of slavery. The years following the Revolution were financially difficult across much of the South. Crops sold for low prices, and farmers struggled to make ends meet. Throughout the region, prices for slaves dropped steadily. Slave owners could only look on helplessly as the value of their investments declined. A few frustrated southerners suggested that their region might benefit by abandoning slavery in favor of a northern-style free labor system.

Some southerners even developed detailed plans to eliminate the institution over time. Virginia planter Ferdinando Fairfax, for instance, published a blueprint for abolishing slavery in 1790; his proposal combined gradual emancipation with the deportation of the newly freed blacks to Africa. Others anticipated that slavery might die a natural death, the victim of moral qualms surrounding the institution and the increasing economic woes of southern planters. "The spirit of the master is abating," wrote a hopeful Thomas Jefferson in 1782, "that of the slave rising from the dust."[17]

The Promise of Cotton

But in 1793 the economics of slavery in the South changed dramatically. The main reason had to do with the cultivation of cotton, a crop that had been widely grown for some time in parts of the South. Southern farmers appreciated how easily cotton grew in the rich soil and long, hot, rainy summers of the South. They also appreciated the high demand for cotton. Manufacturers in the North and in Europe were eager to turn southern cotton into clothing, linens, and other materials.

There was, however, a serious drawback to cotton production. To ready the crop for processing, the seeds first had to be removed from the fibers, a slow and difficult process sometimes known as "cleaning" the cotton. Cleaning even a small amount of cotton could take weeks of intensive labor that left little time for other activities. To clean enough cotton to make a realistic profit on the crop required a small army of laborers, and few planters had access to that many slaves. As a result, most farmers did not devote much land to cotton production.

Slaves are hard at work picking cotton on a plantation in Mississippi. Large-scale cultivation of cotton in the South intensified the region's dependence on slave labor.

Nonetheless, southern planters knew that simplifying the cleaning process could bring them enormous profits. Over the years, mechanically minded farmers had dreamed of developing a cotton gin, a machine to do the work of removing the seeds from the cotton fibers. A few tinkerers did develop simple gins. But these machines were too small and inefficient to speed up production. Until the end of the eighteenth century, the dream of building an effective cotton-cleaning machine remained just that: a dream.

Eli Whitney and King Cotton

In 1792 a Massachusetts teacher named Eli Whitney traveled to South Carolina and took a job tutoring the children of a local planter. While in the South, Whitney heard about the problem of cleaning cotton and set himself to the task of building a better machine. Before long, he developed a gin that seemed much more effective than previous models. Whitney patented a refined version of his machine in 1793.

The Price of Slaves

The price of slaves was subject to the laws of supply and demand, so it fluctuated from year to year and place to place. When times were good, the price of slaves rose; when money was scarce throughout the South, as for instance after a bad cotton harvest, prices often dropped. Over time, however, the purchase price of slaves increased much more often than it decreased. Inflation played a role in the rising prices, but for the most part, slaves represented excellent investments.

The chart below, adapted from Franklin and Moss's *From Slavery to Freedom*, shows the steady rise in the average selling price of slaves in several southern cities between 1800 (soon after the invention of the cotton gin) and 1860.

	1800	1818	1837	1860
Charleston, South Carolina	$500	$850	$1,200	$1,200
Louisville, Kentucky	$400	$800	$1,200	$1,400
New Orleans, Louisiana	$500	$1,000	$1,300	$1,800

Whitney's gin was simple to build and to run, and he was sure it would help the South's cotton producers. "With this Ginn," he boasted, "two persons will clean as much cotton in one Day, as a Hundred persons could cleane in the same time with the gins now in common use."[18] Whitney was right. It soon became evident that one person could clean fifty pounds of cotton a day by using his machine, an enormous improvement over previous machines. Whitney's invention had eliminated the bottleneck in cotton production.

Farmers could now plant as much cotton as they wished, and they proceeded to do exactly that. Over the next few years, southern acreage given over to cotton increased dramatically as farmers converted fields of corn, oats, or tobacco to cotton production instead. Between 1793 and 1800, the amount of cotton produced in the United States quadrupled. By 1815 cotton had become the single most valuable American export. Cotton had risen to a place of unprecedented importance. Indeed, southerners only half-jokingly referred to the crop as "King Cotton."

The Plantation System

More than any other factor, it was the rise of cotton that solidified slavery's hold on the South. The reason was that intensive cotton production required a great deal of labor. Although the cotton gin had eliminated the most difficult and time-consuming task associated with the process, much work still remained.

Slaves use a cotton gin to separate the seeds from the plant's soft fibers. Using Eli Whitney's invention, slaves dramatically increased the rate of cotton production.

Planting, tending, and harvesting the plants took time and energy. Moreover, the growing season for cotton lasted nearly the entire year. As a result, although producing cotton was considerably more lucrative than producing most other crops common to the region, it also required more labor.

The realities of cotton production, therefore, led to an increased demand for slaves. The extra expenses associated with buying and owning more workers were more than offset by the profits that could be realized by expanding the cotton acreage of a farm. Not all farmland was equally conducive to growing cotton, of course, and many planters made the conscious decision to keep planting corn, oats, and other crops on at least some of their fields. Still, the lure of cotton was difficult to resist. Planters who had once struggled to find work for six or eight slaves now took steps to double their labor force.

The growth of cotton production sparked movement west into Alabama and Mississippi—and, later, Louisiana, Texas, and Arkansas. Thousands of Georgians, Virginians, and Carolinians flocked into these new territories in hopes of planting cotton and making a fortune; in a common phrase of the time, they had caught "Alabama fever."[19] The growing demand for laborers in Alabama and other western locales also helped establish slavery as a viable system in the South.

The rise of King Cotton brought with it major changes for the slaves and for southern agriculture in general. At first, many farmers moved enthusiastically into cotton production, paying little heed to the size of their holdings or to the limits of their financial resources. It soon became clear, however, that not all farmers could expect the same return on cotton. In general, cotton production was most efficient—and most profitable—when carried out on a large scale. Cotton production required specialized heavy equipment, for instance, which paid for itself more rapidly the more it was used. Thus, farmers with more land and more slaves tended to do better than those with fewer acres and a smaller labor force.

This natural advantage soon resulted in the development of a new agricultural model. Little by little, successful planters looked to expand their operations. In the more heavily populated states such as South Carolina and Georgia, they bought more land from their neighbors; in the new western territories, they cleared the wilderness and set up farms that sprawled across the countryside. By the 1820s the results of this trend were evident. Though small family-run farms continued to operate, the cotton-growing part of the region was increasingly dominated by large farms known as plantations.

Compared with the small family-run farms, plantations were enormous. The most common definition of a plantation, however, did not rely on the acreage of a farm but on the number of slaves who lived and worked there. To be considered a plantation, a farm had to have at least twenty slaves on the premises; many plantations had considerably more than that. Before the invention of the cotton gin, few slaves had lived on such sizable farms. But when the economics of southern farming changed, so too did the importance of plantations. The change was quick and sweeping. By 1860 well over half of all slaves lived on plantations, and one slave in every four lived on a farm with at least fifty other slaves.

An Organizational Pyramid

Plantations were not only bigger than family-run farms; they also functioned differently. In a sense, plantations were like agricultural factories. They were designed to produce a specific product—cotton—and to do so as profitably as possible. Over the years, planters developed a streamlined system for producing their crop, which soon became standard across the cotton-producing parts of the South. This system required regimentation, organization, and layers of management unknown (and unnecessary) on smaller farms.

The management of a plantation was structured like a pyramid. At the top of the pyramid was the plantation owner, who held title to the land, the slaves, and the other assets of the property. Plantation owners were a varied group. Most lived on the plantation itself, in a well-appointed home that the slaves usually called the "big house." Others were absentee owners who visited their holdings only rarely. Some had made their fortunes recently, during the cotton boom; others had been born to wealth. Most owned just one plantation, but some owned several.

The workings of a large plantation, especially those with more than thirty slaves, were usually too complex for the owner to

Rice and Sugar

◼

The rise of the plantation South was attributable largely to the growth of cotton as a staple crop. But cotton was not the only crop grown on plantations. The plantation system was also used to cultivate two other important southern crops: rice and sugarcane.

Unlike cotton, rice and sugarcane were never widely cultivated through the South. Conditions of soil and climate sharply limited where they could be grown. Most rice plantations were on the coasts of Georgia and South Carolina, where a humid climate and low-lying land combined to create the swampy conditions essential to the crop's development. Sugarcane, meanwhile, needed an exceptionally long growing season and hot weather nearly year-round; growers found Louisiana most suitable for cane production.

Like cotton, however, both rice and sugar were most profitable when they were grown on a large scale. As a result, plantations quickly developed in those parts of the Deep South where these crops were most often cultivated. Rice and sugar plantations were run and structured slightly differently than cotton plantations. Whereas overseers were a constant presence on the cotton fields, for instance, rice planters usually assigned their slaves a specific task, or set of tasks, and had them check in with an overseer only upon the completion of their work. Nonetheless, the basic plantation model—that is, a few owners and overseers managing a large number of slave laborers—remained the same regardless of the crop.

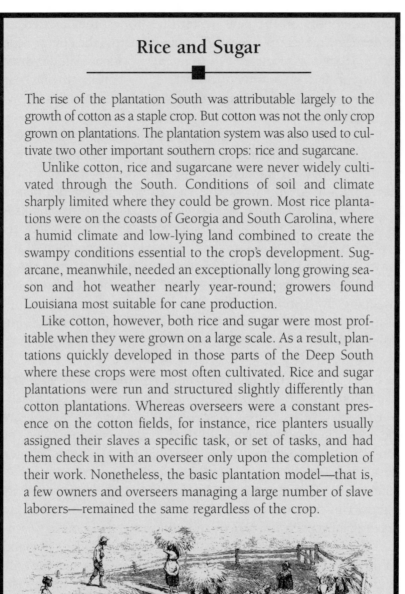

Slaves unload bales of rice transported by barge upriver from the Georgia coast.

manage alone. Thus, owners hired white plantation managers, sometimes called overseers, to make sure the farm ran smoothly; these overseers made up the second layer of the pyramid. The owners usually made the biggest decisions affecting the property, such as when to buy more land or how much cotton to plant. But the managers made the day-to-day decisions that kept the farm in business, such as ordering supplies, preparing crops for transport to market, and determining when to begin the spring planting.

Making these decisions was not the overseer's only task. Most overseers were also expected to supervise the slaves. As one planter wrote, "[An overseer] must always be with the [field]hands when not otherwise engaged in the Employers business."[20] In this capacity, overseers were responsible for getting as much work from the slaves as was possible, regardless of the human cost.

On a small plantation, one overseer could sometimes manage all these tasks. On larger plantations, however, it was impossible for one person to handle the slaves and the business details of the farm. In such cases, owners usually assigned the head overseer all the business responsibilities of running the farm, and hired younger or less skilled overseers to carry out the direct supervision of the slaves. Nearly all plantations with more than one hundred slaves used this model of management, and some smaller ones did as well. Like the managers on smaller plantations, these overseers were charged with pushing the slaves to the limits of their endurance—and sometimes beyond. What was important was profit, not the well-being of the slaves.

The structure and size of plantations led to a new emphasis on regimentation. On small, family-run farms, the slaves worked in a variety of capacities; they did whatever needed to be done, and they did it whenever time permitted. On large plantations, though, this informality was no longer possible. Slaves marched together to the fields each morning and returned together at day's end. They performed one task again and again, day after day, until the season changed; then they moved on to another assignment. Speed and efficiency were essential, and the pace and structure of the day reflected that. "Every thing moves on systematically," wrote a visitor to one Louisiana plantation, "and with the discipline of a regular trained army."[21]

An overseer smokes a pipe as slaves harvest tobacco. It was the overseer's responsibility to ensure the productivity of the slaves he supervised.

A Southern Institution

The most important impact of the plantation system, however, was on the South's commitment to slavery. If slavery, as a southern institution, had ever actually been in danger of dying a gradual death, the rise of cotton—and the rise of the plantation system—had eliminated that possibility. Southern agricultural success rested on the backs of hundreds of thousands of unpaid laborers. The cotton gin had made large-scale cultivation possible, the ambition of planters had led to plantations in Alabama and Arkansas, but the slaves had made King Cotton a reality. Without them, there would have been no economic boom.

As slavery sparked a rise in the South's financial fortunes, southern moral concerns over the rightness of slavery receded. By 1820 few southerners were hoping that southern slavery might die a natural death; fewer still were echoing Washington in describing slavery as evil. Even most southerners who did not own slaves embraced slavery. After all, slavery brought wealth into their region, thereby improving the economic situation of all whites. Moreover, by keeping African Americans in bondage, slavery raised the social status of whites and kept blacks from competing with them for jobs.

By 1860 approximately 4 million slaves lived from Delaware to Texas and from Florida to Missouri. The institution of slavery had become distinctively southern culturally as well as geographically. Southerners pointed with pride to the well-run plantations of their region, to the near-unanimous enthusiasm for slavery among the whites of the South, and to slavery's contributions to southern prosperity. Unfortunately, in doing so, they overlooked the price of slavery, a price that was measured not in dollars and cents but in blood and bondage: the appalling human cost of the peculiar institution.

Chapter Three

The Experience of Slavery

The millions of black men, women, and children who were forced to work for white southerners all had individual experiences of slavery, experiences as varied as the circumstances of each slave's life. Nevertheless, all slaves shared one basic characteristic: They were someone else's property. On some level, it made no difference where individual slaves lived, who their masters were, or what type of job they were assigned. What mattered was that slaves were not free. They could not choose their masters, could not choose their work, and could not choose where and with whom they lived. That reality was central to slaves' daily life, just as it was central to their legal status.

The laws of the South were designed to support the needs of slave owners. Every slave state had a body of laws, known as the slave codes, that regulated the lives of the slaves. The details varied from state to state, but they all affirmed that a slave enjoyed few rights. According to the codes, for instance, slaves could not testify in court against a white person or enter into a contract. Slaves could not possess firearms, leave their plantations without their masters' consent, or strike a white person even in self-defense.

The codes in a few states did enumerate a handful of rights for slaves. In some places, for instance, the law required masters to provide the basics of food and shelter to their slaves. Similarly, some states set legal limits regarding the amount of punishment a slave could receive, though the limits were not always honored and were in any case set extremely high. Still, these provisions were strongly outnumbered by the limitations the laws placed on the slaves' rights. In sum, the slave codes explained, slaves had no power over their own lives. They could be beaten, sold, and worked to exhaustion, and no one would interfere. In the eyes of the law, slaves were not people. They were things.

Work

In addition to being considered a piece of property, nearly every slave experienced slavery in other, more immediate ways. In particular, on a day-to-day basis slavery meant a crushing amount of work. At its heart, slavery was a system of making farming profitable to property owners, and there was no profit in an idle slave.

A group of slaves picks cotton in a plantation field. Daily life for slaves meant hours of backbreaking labor.

Most plantation slaves worked in the fields. The chores assigned these slaves varied with the seasons. On a typical cotton plantation, for instance, slaves plowed the ground early in the winter and planted cotton seeds as the weather grew warmer. During the spring and summer, the workers regularly hoed and weeded the crop. Fall was harvest time, when slaves picked the cotton and prepared it for shipment. Once the harvest was complete, sometimes as late as December, slaves did maintenance work or other tasks until the cycle began again. Other crops had similar patterns.

Whatever the crop and the season, however, there is no question that the vast majority of agricultural slaves worked long hours. Visitors to southern plantations often commented on the amount of time the slaves spent working. So did former slaves looking back on their experiences in slavery. "The night . . . was shortened at both ends," recalled Frederick Douglass, a Maryland slave who escaped from his owner and traveled north to become a prominent antislavery activist. "The slaves worked often as late as they could see . . . and at the first gray streak of morning they were summoned to the fields by the overseer's horn."[22]

The work was exhausting as well. Virtually every aspect of farming involved significant physical labor, which wore down bodies and damaged muscles and skin. Picking cotton, for example, required slaves to bend and stoop to reach the low plants. Moreover, the wads of cotton fiber were protected by sharp thorns that pierced the slaves' fingers. One slave recalled that his fellow laborers picked "till the blood [ran] from the tips of their fingers."[23] Other tasks were not quite so onerous, but few farm chores were easy or relaxing. Even guiding a heavy plow being dragged behind a mule could be tiring, and many slaves were forced to pull the plows themselves.

Not all plantation slaves labored in the fields. A few slaves carried out various tasks in and around the plantation's big house. These men and women were known as house slaves. Women cooked, served as maids, or cared for the masters' children. Men might fill the role of coachman, butler, or gardener. The largest plantations also had slaves working as carpenters, blacksmiths, and other artisans. Given a choice, most slaves preferred to work in the big house, and a division grew on some plantations

For most slaves, being a house servant like this woman ironing her master's shirt was preferable to working in the fields.

between the field hands and the house slaves. "We house slaves thought we wuz better'n the others what worked in the field,"[24] recalled one man.

But being a house slave was not easy. Though their work was less physically taxing, house slaves often worked longer hours than their counterparts in the fields. Indeed, the only slaves from whom no work was expected were the very young, the very old, and the very sick. By the time they reached adolescence, nearly all slaves were expected to shoulder a full workload. And though a few masters did permit a quasi-retirement for their oldest slaves, comparatively few slaves lived that long. In the end, long hours, hard work, and lack of attention to health combined to shorten the life of almost every slave.

Punishment

If work was a constant in the life of nearly every slave, punishment was almost as common. With few exceptions, the laws of the South specified that slaves could be corrected by their masters at any time and for any reason at all. As a rule, the severity of any punishment was left to the owner's discretion. That policy fit

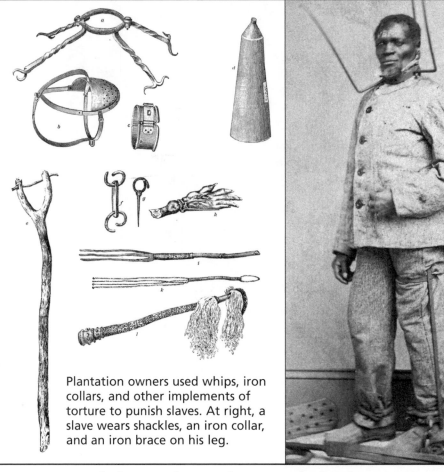

Plantation owners used whips, iron collars, and other implements of torture to punish slaves. At right, a slave wears shackles, an iron collar, and an iron brace on his leg.

in with the prevailing southern attitude that slaves were property. In general, southerners agreed, a master could do what he liked with his property, and the state had no business interfering.

Physical punishment of slaves, therefore was perfectly legal, and most southern planters heartily advocated its use. Many plantation owners and overseers, in fact, saw no realistic alternative. They argued that slaves were naturally lazy and that only violence, or the threat of violence, could get them to work harder. That perspective justified physically punishing slaves who worked slowly or took long rest breaks. Southern leaders also believed that physical punishment served to remind slaves of their masters' power. This idea, in turn, justified the beating of slaves who tried to run away, who talked back to a white person, or who committed any other act that might weaken the owner's control of his or her slaves—and thereby weaken the institution of slavery itself.

Masters employed many different physical punishments. A few slaves, particularly those who had unsuccessfully run away from their masters, were branded. Others were disciplined by being tied or shackled and left for hours under the hot sun. Some slaves had heavy iron chains fastened around their ankles or metal clamps placed on their necks and heads. In short, punishments were limited only by the overseer's willingness to inflict pain. "If we didn't git round [the fields] fast enough," recalled one slave, "[the overseer would] chain us to a tree at night with nothing to eat."[25]

"The Burning Agonies of Hell"

The most common physical punishment for a slave, however, was whipping. The whips most frequently used in the slave South were made from strips of cowhide, with a hooked wire attached to one end. Slaves were forced to lie still or stand while a master or overseer lashed them with the whip. The impact of the cowhide was painful enough; the wire added to the agony by tearing out chunks of flesh. "I thought I must die between the lashes," recalled one man. "My sufferings I can compare to nothing else than the burning agonies of hell!"[26]

Even three or four strokes with the whip could be intensely painful. But few masters stopped so soon. It was not uncommon for slaves to be given fifty, one hundred, or even two hundred strokes at a time. Some slaves received as many as four hundred lashes for a single offense. Though slaves were valuable, masters were not averse to inflicting severe wounds, or in some cases killing their slaves. "I have seen men whipped to death," said one Alabama slave, "have seen them die."[27]

The brutality of such beatings left deep physical marks on those who survived. One master seeking the return of his runaway slave described the man as "much scarred with the whip,"[28] and the same could have been said about thousands of others. Just as important, however, were the emotional scars that whippings left behind. A beating was a clear reminder that slaves were not in control of any part of their lives. "I lays in de bunk two days, gittin' over dat whippin'," recalled a Texas slave, "gittin' over it in de body but not in de heart. No, suh, I has dat in de heart till dis day."[29]

To be sure, not all slaves received physical punishment on a regular basis, and a few never received any at all. Not every master accepted the conventional wisdom that beatings were necessary for every infraction. On some plantations, slaves could escape whippings as long as they were hard workers who generally stayed out of trouble. Likewise, some masters strictly limited the types of punishments they would allow, even in response to serious offenses. "You can correct them for they own good and make them work right," one slave remembered a master telling an overseer, "but you ain't better cut they hide [skin] or draw no blood."[30] Masters like this one, however, were exceptions.

Sexual abuse of slave women by white men was another form of violence on many southern plantations. Sometimes this abuse took the form of outright rape, in which a master, a master's son, or an overseer forced himself on an unwilling and resisting female slave. Although it is not possible at this point to quantify the frequency of such abuse, it is clear from anecdotal evidence that the raping of slave women was a fact of life on many plantations. In an atmosphere of violence and brutality, where slaves were seen as things and not people, at least some southern men saw themselves as fully justified in taking slave women by force.

Sexual abuse in the plantation South could also be much more subtle. Many white men used slave women as mistresses. These relationships often did not involve outright violence, direct force, or spoken threats. Nonetheless, they were far from fully consensual. Slave women, after all, had no legal right to refuse the advances of their white owners. Although theoretically they could have done so, they knew that protesting would likely bring them severe and brutal punishment. Under the circumstances, most saw accepting the advances as the safest course.

From beatings to sexual abuse, violence directed toward slaves was all too common across the plantation South. Almost every slave suffered from brutality at some point during his or her life. And even those slaves who received little or no physical punishment nevertheless lived in constant fear of a beating. The promise of violence was a central part of the slaves' existence; it colored

Plantation owners routinely beat disobedient slaves. From beatings to sexual abuse, acts of violence committed on slaves were very common on southern plantations.

all of their actions and all of their thoughts. Violence and brutality were simply part of the experience of being enslaved.

The Necessities of Life

Just as punishments and workloads varied from plantation to plantation, so too did the type and quality of the food, clothing, and shelter the slaves were given. Northern antislavery activists often charged that slaves lacked many of these basic necessities. But leading southern slaveholders denied the charges and insisted that slave owners provided their workers with everything they needed. "The slaves are all well fed," explained Virginia planter George Fitzhugh, "well clad, have plenty of fuel, and are happy."[31]

Fitzhugh's assertion was roughly accurate for at least some slaves. "We had plenty to eat," recalled one slave. "Whoooo-ee! Just plenty to eat."[32] Some owners specified that their slaves

Slave Gardens

———————◼———————

Slaves were often allowed to grow vegetables and other crops in gardens of their own, and despite the time it took to maintain these plots of land, many slaves were delighted to do so. The vegetables they raised helped supplement their sometimes meager and unvaried diets. Moreover, many slaves appreciated having a plot of land they could call their own (even if it technically belonged to the master) and a chance to work on a project that benefited them, not their owners, directly.

But then, those slaveholders who permitted gardening benefited, too. Every ear of corn produced in these gardens and eaten by a slave family meant one fewer ear that the master had to provide. The gardens also took up much of the slaves' free time, which planters feared might otherwise be spent in causing trouble. And some slave owners noted that gardens and similar projects helped keep slaves rooted to their homes. A slave who invested dozens of hours in creating a garden, they pointed out, was a slave who was less likely to try to run away.

should receive a variety of foods, even if the financial situation on the plantation was bleak. Others ordered overseers to make sure that slave cabins were dry, clean, and well aired. A few plantation owners likewise took pains to ensure that their slaves had sufficient clothing to protect them from rain, cold, and the heat of the sun.

Nevertheless, for the majority of slaves, Fitzhugh's opinion was very far from the mark. On many plantations, miserly or selfish masters gave slaves less food than they needed; forced them to live in drafty, tumbledown shacks; and offered clothing that did not adequately shield them from the elements. The slaves did the best they could with what they were given, often working on their own time to supplement their masters' offerings. But even so, most slaves suffered from inadequate food, shelter, and clothing.

"The Dogs Got Better Eating"

Food was a particular concern. Slaves generally received a steady diet of a few staple foods such as cornmeal and fatty bacon, a diet that was bland, boring, and nutritionally suspect at best. "Why, the dogs got better eating than we poor colored folks,"[33] complained a Georgia slave. Worse, many masters sharply limited the amount of food they provided, so slaves frequently went hungry. "There never was as much as we needed,"[34] one woman lamented.

Some slaves did find ways of adding to their meager diet. Many slaves fished for extra food, and others used traps and clubs to kill small wild animals for meat. Gardens were common, too, and many slaves took great pride in the vegetables they grew for personal use. In a pinch, slaves would gladly take food from their masters. On some plantations, especially those where rations were consistently small, no storehouse, chicken coop, or pigpen was safe from slaves eager to "liberate" the food within. The slaves who took part in these raids did so at great personal risk, but sometimes the necessity of fresh, tasty food outweighed the need for caution.

Like food, slave housing was usually inadequate. Plantation owners provided their slaves with cabins that usually measured

A slave family poses in front of their dilapidated home in South Carolina. Slave houses were poorly constructed dwellings that provided an extremely cramped living space.

Distribution of Slavery

———■———

Although slavery was a southern institution by 1800, it was never spread equally across the entire region. In some areas, notably the Upper South—the northernmost tier of slave-holding states—and the mountainous parts of Tennessee, Virginia, and North Carolina, slavery was not at all common. In 1860 for example, there were fewer than two thousand slaves in the entire state of Delaware. Some counties in these areas had no more than a few dozen slaves, if that. Slavery was actually in decline in a few places: The number of slaves in Maryland, for instance, gradually dropped during the late 1850s.

On the other hand, in some parts of the South slavery was prevalent. This was particularly true in the Deep South, where most plantations were located. In South Carolina, for example, slaves outnumbered the state's white population during the years of plantation slavery. Many counties in Alabama and Louisiana had ratios of two or three slaves for every white resident. And in parts of Mississippi, the situation was even more dramatic: In the counties that produced the most cotton, slaves made up nine-tenths of the population. The variances in numbers and proportions of slaves alone suggest that the experience of slavery was different in many ways between one part of the South and the next.

about twelve feet square and were shared by two families. Poor construction was a regular feature of most of these dwellings. One Mississippi planter wrote of "the decaying logs . . . open floors, leaky roofs, and crowded rooms"[35] that prevailed in slave cabins throughout his region. When they could, slaves chinked the walls with mud and moss, and many strived to keep their quarters clean and neat, but they had little to work with.

Clothing was similarly inadequate. Most slaves lacked shoes, and many had no clothing heavy enough to protect them from the winter cold. Some had no hats to ward off the sun in hot weather. The occasional shirts, pants, and dresses issued to the slaves were made of coarse, uncomfortable cloth that wore out quickly; nonetheless, masters were reluctant to provide better materials, and replaced tattered clothing only rarely. Northern visitors to the South were often shocked to see slaves clad in rags or even less. It was not that the slaves chose to be naked. Their masters simply had not seen fit to provide them with clothes.

Substandard housing, clothing, and food, in short, were central to the experience of most slaves. When discussing the horrors of slavery, former slaves usually began by citing the brutality, the humiliation, and the workload associated with the system, but many also mentioned their sorrow and frustration at being denied basic necessities. The words of planters like George Fitzhugh notwithstanding, being a slave meant being forced to endure these deprivations.

Family Life

Being a slave also meant coping with other laws and customs, both large and small, each one a reminder that slaves had no control over their lives. Because southern leaders thought it advisable to keep their slaves ignorant of the world around them, for instance, it was illegal in most slave states to teach a slave to read and write. Many masters offered their slaves only the most rudimentary medical care. And slaves were required to obey the orders of virtually any white person, including even very young children.

Perhaps the most difficult issues, however, involved families. At every turn, the realities of the plantation South prevented slaves from having a normal family life. Slaves married, or at least they chose mates and participated in informal wedding ceremonies. But since slaves could not enter into contracts, these marriages had no legal standing. Slaves had babies and raised children, but masters, not the parents, were the ultimate authorities over these young slaves. And even though children were among the few sources of joy available to slaves, work hours were so long that most slave families had little time to spend together.

What most threatened family life among slaves, however, was the reality that a master could at any time sell one member of a family. Despite claims of southern apologists that such sales were very rare, the historical record shows that thousands of slave families were indeed separated by sale. In many cases, the separation was permanent, and family members never saw one another again. Historians note that many masters did their best to avoid selling a husband away from a wife or parents away from their children. But not all tried to avoid it, and not all succeeded.

The apologists were wrong about another aspect of these sales, too. Although a South Carolina planter named James Hammond contended that the few slaves sold away from their families were "comparatively indifferent"[36] to their fate, the statements of slaves completely contradict this assertion. Indeed, some of the most tragic accounts of slavery are the recollections of slaves who were separated from spouses, parents, or children. "I've got one child who is buried in Kentucky, and that grave is pleasant to think of," said a slave who had escaped to Canada. "I've got another that is sold nobody knows where, and that I never can bear to think of."[37]

A slave family in Virginia is placed on the auction block. Slave families were sometimes broken up at auction, with the individual slaves sold to the highest bidder.

The Domestic Slave Trade

William Wells Brown was a Missouri slave who successfully ran away to the North in 1834. Prior to his escape, Brown had served on a steamboat that plied the Mississippi and Ohio rivers. At one point, he was assigned to help prepare slaves for purchase at a New Orleans slave market. His experience appears in this excerpt from Gilbert Osofsky's *Puttin' On Ole Massa*.

> In a short time, the planters came flocking to the pen to purchase slaves. Before the slaves were exhibited for sale, they were dressed and driven out into the yard. Some were set to dancing, some to jumping, some to singing, and some to playing cards. This was done to make them appear cheerful and happy. My business was to see that they were placed in those situations before the arrival of the purchasers, and I have often set them to dancing when their cheeks were wet with tears. As slaves were in good demand at that time, they were all soon disposed of.

In the end, the possibility of such a sale was always present. Even otherwise considerate masters were known to break up families. Financial pressures, for example, sometimes led an owner to sell individual slaves to the highest bidder, even if doing so separated a family. Like hard work, the threat of punishment, and insufficient food, clothing, and shelter, the risk of family breakup was a fundamental part of the experience of slavery. These fears, frustrations, and hardships constituted the great tragedy of slavery in the plantation South.

Chapter Four

Challenges from Within

The legal and social systems of the plantation South were designed to help the planters maintain strict control over the slaves. To a great extent, these measures worked just as the slaveholders hoped. But the power of the slaveholder was not unlimited. No planter, however controlling, could be everywhere at once; no overseer, however eagle-eyed, could observe every slave's actions throughout the course of the day. Moreover, slaves were thinking, feeling human beings, beaten down but not defeated by the system that brutalized and oppressed them. In ways great and small, many slaves were willing to challenge their masters—and the institution of slavery itself.

Avoidance and Rascality

Slaves knew that their value lay in the work they did. Thus, many slaves reasoned, the best way of fighting back against the slave system was to do as little work as possible. Few slaves directly challenged the authority of a master or an overseer to require them to work, and with good reason: A slave who simply refused to work could expect a swift and severe punishment. But many slaves were poised to challenge their masters indirectly, in subtle ways that were difficult to detect.

One very simple method of avoiding work, for instance, relied on the fact that one overseer could monitor only a few slaves at once. Typically, slaves who wanted to reduce their workload kept careful track of their overseer's movements. When the overseer was close by, the slaves would work productively and with apparent enthusiasm. When he moved off to another part of the field, however, the slaves abruptly slowed their pace. If they dared, they might even stop working altogether until the overseer returned.

Slaves also found ways of appearing to do more work than they actually did. During the cotton harvest, for instance, each slave was usually assigned a specific number of pounds to pick before being allowed to go home. Usually, it took slaves the entire day to reach their assigned weight. But some slaves put rocks in the bottoms of their baskets or wet some of the cotton to make it

Slaves hoe rows of soil in a cotton field as an overseer looks on. In the overseer's absence, some slaves stopped working altogether.

appear heavier than it actually was. Not only did these slaves enjoy a less arduous day of picking, but they had the additional satisfaction of fooling their masters.

Perhaps more subtle still—and certainly more annoying to the planters—was the degree to which slaves avoided work by feigning incompetence. In general, slaves were quite capable of doing the tasks they were assigned. But it was often to their advantage to act otherwise. When given direct orders, for example, slaves sometimes pretended not to understand what the master wanted. Or they would accept their orders and then delay carrying them out. Every minute the master spent repeating the instruction or demonstrating the task was a minute during which the slave did not have to work.

It was an article of faith among southern planters that whites were superior to blacks socially, morally, and, most of all, intellectually. More than one southern thinker wrote of the mental inferiority of blacks as though it were a scientific fact. Thus, many masters assumed that these slaves really were as incompetent as they appeared. But slave testimony contradicts this view, as do the recollections of more thoughtful masters. These masters referred to the feigned incompetence as "rascality," and they knew exactly what game the slaves were playing. In most cases, though, they were powerless to put a complete stop to it.

Destruction and Shamming

Pretense could take more damaging forms, too. Sometimes, for instance, slaves pretended not to know how to handle valuable tools. Deliberately, but apparently innocently, they misused and damaged axes, plows, wagons, and other equipment. As one frustrated planter complained, slaves "break and destroy more farming utensils, ruin more carts, break more gates . . . and commit more waste than five times the number of white laborers do."[38] Slaves sometimes enjoyed periods of idleness while replacement equipment was sought, and once again they gained some satisfaction by irritating the master.

Shamming, or feigning illness or injury, was yet another way in which slaves successfully evaded their tasks. Though masters could often be quite brutal, they did not usually take the chance of making a possibly sick slave sicker. Slaves cost too much money not to err on the side of caution. A few slaves—especially women, with their poorly defined "female troubles"—managed to feign illness for a week or even longer, but most shammers did not try to keep up the charade for more than a day or so. It was hard to maintain nonexistent symptoms past that time, and masters became more suspicious of the genuineness of the illness the longer it lasted.

Still, even a day's respite was better than nothing. Like the slaves who loaded their cotton sacks with rocks and those who pretended not to understand directions, the slaves who feigned illness were sparing themselves work, costing their owners money, and fooling the whites who ran their plantations. Whether consciously or not, all of them were fighting back against an oppressive system.

Fugitive Slaves

Most slaves never went beyond rascality and shamming in their attempt to undermine their masters. Some slaves, though, took on the institution of slavery more directly and more dramatically. These were the fugitive slaves, or, as white southerners referred to them, the runaways. The goal of these men and women was to escape altogether from their plantations and the influence of their masters.

To escape from slavery was the ultimate in avoiding work, of course, but it meant much more. Though most fugitive slaves acted solely for personal reasons, every attempt to run away also functioned as a blow to the heart of the slave system. Fugitive slaves were proof that slaves did not prefer enslavement, as many southern apologists insisted they did. Fugitive slaves were evidence that brutality and fear, despite the conventional wisdom of southern planters, did not serve to make all blacks meek and obedient. Instead, these slaves were responding to their condition by leaving it behind. They were acting like free people, and they were determined to become exactly that.

Running away, of course, was extremely difficult for nearly all slaves. During daylight hours, slaves were closely supervised and rarely left alone for long. Leaving under cover of darkness gave slaves a head start, but slave patrols, armed groups of whites who roamed the countryside at night in search of runaways, were a

A white man armed with a whip cries out as his dog forces a fugitive slave from his hiding place.

constant danger. An escaping slave captured by the patrols could expect a violent beating, or worse. Other barriers to escape included slaves' sketchy knowledge of the surrounding countryside; thickets, swamps, and other difficult terrain; and the need to find adequate food and shelter without being revealed.

Many slaves, upon fleeing from their plantations, had no particular destination in mind. Most of these simply sought out a hiding place close to their former homes. They holed up in nearby swamps and forests, living off the land or—in some cases—regularly sneaking back to their plantations to get food from slaves who had stayed behind. Some runaways lived this way for years. In South Carolina, for instance, one group of patrollers stumbled on a backcountry settlement populated entirely by fugitive slaves. The runaways had been there for some time, the patrollers reported. They had begun to raise vegetables, and their shelters, reported one member of the patrol, were "well provided with meal, cooking utensils, blankets, etc."[39]

Heading North

The fugitives' best chance of permanent freedom, though, typically lay in journeying to a more distant destination: the North. Although most slaves had little geographic knowledge, they generally knew that slavery was forbidden both in the northern part of the United States and in the neighboring country of Canada. If they could travel that far, the slaves reasoned, they might not have to fear recapture. Some were willing to die to achieve that freedom. "There's two things I've got a right to," said runaway slave Harriet Tubman, who escaped to Pennsylvania in 1849, "and those are Death and Liberty. . . . No one will take me back alive."[40]

Reaching the North was mentally and physically taxing. As long as they remained in the South, slaves had to stay out of sight or run a serious risk of being captured, beaten, and sent home. Runaways therefore traveled mainly by night, using the North Star to help them stay on course. They ate whatever food was available, and they grabbed bits of sleep whenever they could. Despite the hardships, though, the fugitives pushed forward. "When I thought of . . . the prospect of liberty before me," remembered one runaway, "my heart was strengthened, and I forgot that I was tired or hungry."[41]

Some slaves undertook such journeys entirely on their own. Others had help from friends, family, or even strangers, who covertly offered shelter and food to fugitives and directed them to others who could help. During the nineteenth century, a loose confederation of former slaves, northern abolitionists, and anti-slavery southerners set up a network known as the Underground Railroad. Formed strictly for the purpose of guiding runaways to

"Slaves He . . . Never Could See"

One of the most remarkable stories about runaway slaves concerns a Kentucky slave named Arnold Gragston. Born on Christmas Day, 1840, Gragston belonged to a master named Jack Tabb, whom he described as "a pretty good man" (quoted in B.A. Botkin's *Lay My Burden Down*). Gragston appreciated that he received relatively rare beatings from Tabb, and he was pleased that Tabb allowed his slaves to learn to read and write. But mainly, Gragston liked the fact that Tabb did not monitor the slaves actions carefully.

Gragston lived near the banks of the Ohio River, so he was only a short boat ride from the free northern states. On a visit to a nearby plantation one night, Gragston was asked whether he might be able to ferry a young female slave across the river to freedom. After some thought, Gragston agreed. "I don't know how I ever rowed that boat across the river," Gragston recalled later. "The current was strong, and I was trembling. I couldn't see a thing there in the dark, but I felt that girl's eyes." Still, he rowed to the opposite bank, where two men—probably conductors on the Underground Railroad—appeared from the bushes and hurried the girl to safety.

Gragston never saw the girl again, but the incident changed his life. Word quickly traveled through northern Kentucky about the young slave who had access to a boat and the courage to bring others safely to the opposite shore. "I soon found myself going back across the river," Gragston recalled years later, "with two or three people, and sometimes a whole boatload. I got so I used to make three and four trips a month."

For the next four years, Gragston chose to remain a slave so that he could ferry other slaves to freedom. Only when the Civil War was nearly at an end did he free himself. Moving to Detroit, he fathered ten children and became grandfather to thirty-one. "The bigger ones don't care so much about hearing it now," he said years afterward, "but the little ones never get tired of hearing how their grandpa brought emancipation to loads of slaves he could touch and feel, but never could see."

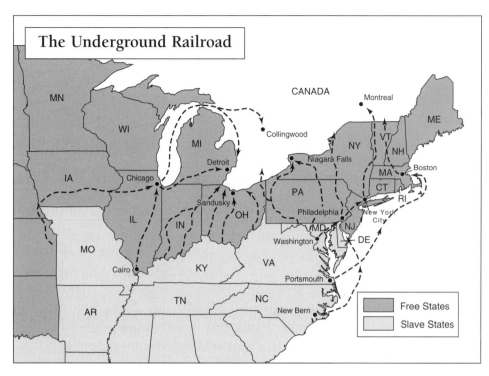

The Underground Railroad

safety, the Underground Railroad helped many hundreds of slaves achieve their freedom. "If it had not been for them," noted a Virginia slave who fled to Canada, "I would not have got here."[42]

Southern plantation owners did their best to recapture all fugitive slaves. They sent patrollers with bloodhounds into nearby forests and swamps in search of runaways. They put out advertisements offering rewards for the escapees' returns. They had the power, the money, and the weapons, and quite often they were able to track down the slaves who ran off. But they did not always find the runaways. During the mid–nineteenth century, at least a thousand slaves a year—and perhaps many more than that—successfully made their way to the North and freedom. The courage and steadfastness of these fugitives brought them the liberty they so desperately wanted—and defied the institution that tried to keep them down.

Slave Violence

The ultimate challenge to slaveholders' authority, however, came not from fugitive slaves but from those slaves who responded to slavery with violence of their own. Such responses, to be sure, were rare. Nearly all slaves were careful to keep their anger and hostility to themselves rather than lashing out physically against a master or an overseer. But now and then, slaves gave in to their frustration and let loose their rage. In such cases, the outcome could be deadly. One slave reported that a fellow field hand, whipped one time too often, "knocked the overseer in the head with a big stick and then took a ax and cut off [the overseer's] hands and feet."[43]

Such episodes of aggression were usually spontaneous and isolated. Occasionally, though, slaves took the time to plan a violent response to the cruelty of their condition. The methods used by these slaves were often extremely subtle. House slaves, for example, were known to poison the food of their masters. Others set fire to the big house at night, hoping that the flames would spread before the family could be evacuated. How common such incidents were is debatable. There is no doubt, though, that southern whites were aware that a determined slave *could* kill them, and this possibility was seldom far from the minds of the slaveholders.

But being killed by a disgruntled house servant or field hand did not represent the deepest nightmare of the southern slave owner. What southern whites feared above all else, instead, was an organized revolt. They dreaded the possibility that dozens, perhaps thousands, of slaves would rise up as a group against their masters. Some especially anxious southerners saw potential slave conspiracies everywhere they turned. "All at once, in Kentucky, Tennessee, Missouri, Arkansas, Louisiana, and Texas," reported one Richmond newspaper shortly before the Civil War, "it is discovered that the slaves are meditating schemes of insurrection."[44]

The truth, however, was that organized slave revolts were so rare they were almost nonexistent. The most famous one took place in Virginia in 1831, when a slave preacher named Nat Turner led a few followers in a sudden and unexpected uprising. Acting swiftly, Turner and his men killed about sixty whites in two days before scattering into the woods. An enormous manhunt ensued. In the end, Turner and his followers were captured and executed, as were a number of other slaves who had no involvement in, nor knowledge of, the rebellion.

Nat Turner's Rebellion

Nat Turner, the leader of the most successful slave revolt in American history, was born in 1800 on a Virginia farm. Deeply religious from a very early age, he became a preacher and led worship services for his fellow slaves.

At some point, he became convinced that he had been chosen to carry out God's work on earth. Specifically, as he told the story later, he believed that God had assigned him to fight the evils of slavery. "The great day of judgment was at hand," Turner recalled, quoted in *Africans in America* by Charles Johnson and Patricia Smith. "I should arise and prepare myself, and slay my enemies with their own weapons." He experienced visions in which, Turner reported, "I saw white spirits and black spirits engaged in battle, and the sun was darkened . . . and I heard a voice saying, 'Such is your luck, such you are called to see, and let it come rough or smooth, you must surely bear it.'"

On the night of August 21, 1831, Turner and a few trusted followers climbed up a ladder and slipped through a window into his master's home. Turner and his men murdered all five members of the family as they slept, including an infant; then they moved on to neighboring houses. Turner and a force of about forty rebels killed about sixty whites before the

insurrection was put down two days later. Turner escaped capture till October 30, and was executed on November 11.

Nat Turner is captured after he and a band of slaves murdered close to sixty whites.

Turner's was not the only revolt. Other slave rebellions did erupt from time to time. In 1739, for instance, about twenty slaves joined forces to carry out the Stono Rebellion, which resulted in the deaths of perhaps two dozen South Carolina whites. More often, slaves planned revolts which were prevented from taking place by white authorities who learned of the plans. An uprising planned by Virginia slave Gabriel Prosser in 1800, for instance, failed in just this way. And in 1822, South Carolina rebel Denmark Vesey's attempt to stage a general revolt was also thwarted by a slave who alerted his master to the plot.

Realistically the odds that a revolt would succeed were exceptionally low. Even Turner's rebellion, the most effective of all slave revolts, was doomed from the start. The reality of the plantation South was that all power belonged to the whites. Though a rebel such as Turner could wreak significant damage before whites could determine what was happening, there was no way that a slave revolt could hold off the whites for long. White southerners held the weapons, controlled the transportation and communication systems, and outnumbered the slaves by an overall margin in the South of more than two to one. An attack on the system, however effective it might be in the short run, was suicidal in the end.

Still, Turner, Prosser, Vesey, and the others who plotted to revolt had an impact that went far beyond success or failure. The Turner uprising, in particular, shook slave owners from one end of the South to the other. More than any other event of the early nineteenth century, it contradicted the assurances of slaveholders who held that slavery was a benign and kindly institution. In the wake of Turner's revolt, whites could not help wondering privately if their own slaves, or those of their neighbors, might soon emulate Turner by turning against them.

What mattered to southern whites, then, was not so much whether uprisings did happen but whether they *could* take place, and thoughtful southerners, at least, had to admit that the threat of violent insurrection was ever-present. The odds that a revolt would succeed in the long run were astronomically small. Nat Turner, in attacking slavery head-on, had killed only a few dozen whites, and he had paid for his actions with his life. Still, he had thrown a scare into slave owners and challenged the slaveholders' system in a way unmatched by any other slave.

Challenging the institution of slavery, in turn, had an effect that went beyond the experiences of any one slave. Those who ran away, those who plotted a rebellion, even those who found a way to evade an hour or two of work were taking a stand, great or small, against the evils of the slave system. The myriad acts of resistance on southern plantations were a reminder that the oppression of slavery could not extinguish the slaves' essential humanity. They signaled that slaves would not accept their fate without a struggle. Most important of all, in the words of historian Deborah Gray White, resistance "proved to contemporary and future generations that although enslaved, African Americans were fit for freedom."[45]

Chapter Five

Creating a Culture

The plantation system was designed in part to deny the full humanity of the slave. It sought to reduce slaves to the status of children or even property. It was set up to foster the dependence of slaves on their masters. And for the most part, it did exactly that. By working slaves to exhaustion, by beating them on a regular basis, and by refusing to allow them to make even the simplest of decisions, slaveholders asserted their power over their slaves.

Somewhat ironically, however, the plantation system itself also served to undermine some of the slaveholders' goals. In particular, the realities of plantation life helped spark the formation of a uniquely African American culture. The rise of this culture did not represent a direct attack on the institution of slavery, but it did offer the slaves self-respect, a feeling of community, and a renewed sense of their own humanity. In all these ways, the formation of this new culture helped the slaves to bear their burdens.

African Influences

The first Africans who came to what is now the United States arrived with a rich cultural heritage of values and religious beliefs, stories and songs, crafts and festivals. The culture of British North America was strikingly different, and at first most new slaves held tightly to as many of their old ways as they could. In some cases, that was a long time indeed. Even in 1860, two centuries after slavery had been established across the South, it was easy to see African influences and customs among the slaves. A few aspects of African culture, to be sure, had entirely disappeared. Tribal languages had long since vanished, and distinctively African religious beliefs had been replaced by a widespread acceptance of Christianity. Nevertheless, slaves continued to practice dozens of African ways and customs.

On one level, the survival of these customs might seem unexpected. Many immigrant groups, after all, gradually lose their distinctive cultural traditions over time. In addition, colonial slavery was not always favorable to the continuance of African cultural ideas. Because most slaves lived on small farms during this period, there were no large groups of slaves to help keep cultural traditions alive. On the contrary, most slaves were exposed primarily to white European ideas and values. Indeed, many masters, eager to make their slaves docile and dependent, made a conscious effort to destroy the slaves' African cultural roots.

Then again, the slaves were not typical immigrants, and their connections with whites were sharply limited by law and by custom. The slaves' race and status denied them full participation in European American culture. Slaves were kept from voting, from learning to read and write, from forming stable marriages, and

Africans in the Congo pose in traditional dress in this illustration. Once in America, slaves were usually required to wear typical American clothing instead of traditional costume.

from taking part in hundreds of other activities that white Americans took more or less for granted. Barred from entering the mainstream of white American life, slaves fell back on traditions of their own, traditions passed down through the generations and originating in Africa itself.

"A Sort of Weird Chant"

From crafts to child-rearing practices, African influences on slave culture were widespread throughout the plantation South. At festivals and holidays, such as the end-of-the-year celebration known variously as Johnkannaus, Jonkonnu, or John's Canoe, slaves performed dances drawn from West African traditions and wore costumes that reflected African tastes and styles. Folklore, too, was an indication of the ties between Africa and slave culture. For instance, the slaves' tales of Brer (Brother) Rabbit, who used trickery and wit to escape his enemy Brer Fox, had parallels in stories found among many West African peoples.

Nowhere did the connection between slave life and African origins seem more apparent, however, than in the music of the slaves. The ears of many white listeners struggled to make sense of the unfamiliar sounds produced by slave singers and instrumentalists. Although most whites enjoyed slave music, they found much of it unusual and alien. One plantation owner described the music of her slaves as "a sort of weird chant that makes me feel all out of myself when I hear it in the night."[46]

Slave music contained important elements drawn from the slaves' African roots. The complex rhythms of African American drumming, for instance, were based on African models. So were certain vocal techniques, such as the "slides from one note to another" and the "odd turns made in the throat"[47] described by one visitor to South Carolina. And many slave owners saw a clear connection between West African musical instruments and the instruments of the slaves. "The instrument proper to [the slaves] is the Banjar," wrote Thomas Jefferson, using a spelling of *banjo* common at the time, "which they brought hither from Africa."[48]

A Mix of Influences

However, slave music was not nearly as distinctively African as whites sometimes believed. White southerners made music, too,

Messages and Spirituals

Slave spirituals, first and foremost, were sung for religious reasons. Some, such as "Joshua Fit [Fought] the Battle of Jericho," were retellings of stories from the Bible. Others, such as "Swing Low, Sweet Chariot," presented Christian imagery that particularly touched the slaves.

Not all spirituals, however, were sung specifically as expressions of religious feelings. A few had double meanings known only to the slaves. On the surface, for instance, the slave song "I Am Bound for the Land of Canaan" was simply a song about going to heaven. To some slaves, however, "heaven" had a second meaning: freedom and the North. Frederick Douglass, for one, remembered singing this spiritual while planning his escape. The song's secondary meaning alerted Douglass's fellow slaves to his plans without allowing masters or overseers to know what was going on.

"I Am Bound for the Land of Canaan" was only one of several spirituals that not only described the slaves' longing for freedom but also signaled their readiness to leave. "Go Down, Moses" was another. The fugitive slave Harriet Tubman, one of the most famous conductors on the Underground Railroad, frequently returned to the South to help guide more fugitives to safety. For this, she was known as the Moses of her people. In parts of Maryland, slaves secretly told one another that Tubman was nearby by singing "Go Down, Moses."

Slaves clap their hands as they sing a spiritual. The lyrics of these songs expressed the slaves' desire for freedom, either in this world or the afterlife.

Cultural Blending

Just as slave culture incorporated many elements of European traditions, so too was southern white culture affected by the ways of African Americans. Slave music was one clear example: The banjo, for instance, got its start in America as a specifically African instrument, but it soon made its way into the folk culture of the white South as well. Food was another: When African Americans cooked, they often created dishes new to European palates. On some plantations, slave women did the cooking, introducing whites to foods and cooking styles more associated with Africa than with the British Isles. Language was a third area in which African ideas affected southern whites. "Many foreign visitors who came to the South in the nineteenth century," reports historian Nathan Irvin Huggins in *Black Odyssey*, "remarked that English in the South had much to do with black influence."

A group of slaves in Virginia listens to a man playing banjo. Brought from Africa, the banjo quickly became an integral part of southern white folk culture.

and the racial divide that prevailed in the South could not prevent the slaves from hearing and absorbing the music of their masters. Slaves heard Protestant hymns from the rich choral traditions of England and Germany, fiddle tunes native to the Virginia countryside, and folk ballads from Scotland and Ireland. The music of European Americans was in the air of the plantation South; over time, the slaves came to adopt many aspects of this musical style as well.

In fact, in some ways the music of the slaves was more obviously linked to Europe than it was to Africa. Slave musicians quickly learned to play Western-style instruments, such as fiddles, in addition to banjos and drums. By the nineteenth century, the universal language of slave songs was English. Slave spirituals, or religious songs—such as "Michael, Row the Boat Ashore" or "Swing Low, Sweet Chariot"—relied heavily on Christian images unknown to the slaves' West African ancestors. And slave music also utilized harmonic rules, melodic ideas, and structural elements common to the music of white southerners. Strange as white Americans often found the music of the slaves, black Africans of the same period might well have found it stranger still.

In truth, by the nineteenth century slave music was neither African nor European. What defined the music—and indeed, much of the culture of the slaves—was its blending of black Africa and white America. The rich mix of ideas and traditions represented by the slaves' music looked simultaneously back to Africa and ahead to life on the American continent. A uniquely African American culture was emerging on the plantations of the American South.

African Values, American Lives

Nearly all expressions of this new African American culture had clear parallels in both Africa and the United States. In some cases, African and European practices existed more or less side by side. On most plantations, for instance, slaves celebrated both the African-influenced festival of Johnkannaus and the European holiday of Christmas. The slaves celebrated Christmas much as their owners did, with feasts, presents, and family time; nearly all planters gave their slaves a short vacation to mark the holiday. Slaves saw no need to choose between Johnkannaus and Christmas; they were delighted to make both a part of their lives.

More often, however, European and African customs blended seamlessly into something new and different. The dances of slaves are a good example. Traditional African dance steps and movements were popular throughout the plantation era. When slaves learned the steps of popular European dance forms such as reels and schottisches, they replaced some of the standard European steps and movements with dance elements from their own tradition. The end result suggested Africa just as much as the big house. Thus, these "European" dances had become an original expression of slave culture. "Afro-Americans did to conventional European dance what they would do to Methodist hymns," sums up historian Nathan Irvin Huggins. "They adapted them, but in the process converted them to something that was uniquely their own."[49]

Sometimes, slaves reworked African customs to fit the realities of life in America. Slave crafts such as basketry are a good example. The first blacks who arrived in America brought with them traditional methods for weaving baskets from certain reeds and plants. Because these plants were unavailable in America, the slaves were forced to use plants native to the region instead. The different kind of plants led to changes in the color, size, and style of the baskets constructed by the slaves. After several generations, the slaves were producing baskets that were neither African nor American. The baskets, too, had become a unique expression of African American culture.

In a few cases, the blending of cultures was a direct result of the reality of slavery. The Brer Rabbit stories, for example, were of particular interest to the slaves precisely because they were slaves. The stories of the clever little rabbit touched them in ways that many other West African tales did not. Even though Brer Rabbit could not neutralize the powerful teeth and claws of Brer Fox, he could use his guile to defeat his enemy. It was not hard to see that the fox represented the slaveholders and the plucky rabbit reminded the slaves of themselves. The origins of the tales, to be sure, were African, but they survived in a thoroughly American context.

Slave Religion

Perhaps the most obvious example of this blending of African and American cultures was the religious expression of the slaves. The earliest slaveholders were generally content to allow their slaves to practice whatever religion they chose; accordingly, the first slaves often adhered to traditional African faiths. Even as early as the late 1600s, however, some slaveholders were making a concerted attempt to convert their slaves to Christianity. Missionary zeal was part of the reason; most Christians of the time were eager to spread their religion. But the extinguishing of

African religious practices also served to help the slaveholders consolidate their power over the slaves.

By the early 1800s the attempts of these slaveholders had been successful. While religions practiced in Africa had largely vanished, Christianity had become a central part of black identity in the plantation South. When they looked back on their years in slavery, former slaves frequently spoke of the range and depth of their religious feelings and convictions, as well as the amount of time they spent in worship. For many, religion was a comfort and a source of joy. "Sometimes us sing and pray all night,"[50] recalled one former slave.

Not all masters allowed their slaves to attend religious services. "Church?" asked one ex-slave who was forced to spend Sundays doing the washing. "Shucks, we-uns don't know what that mean."[51]

Able to outwit the brute Brer Fox time and time again, the cunning Brer Rabbit was a very appealing character to slaves.

But most plantation owners encouraged slaves to practice Christianity. Some masters hired white ministers to lead the slaves in worship. Others permitted slave preachers to hold services for their fellow workers. Even slaves whose masters officially forbade religious services often found ways of worshipping in secret. Thus, few slaves of the plantation era were wholly ignorant of Christianity.

In many ways, the slaves' expression of Christianity was much like that of their masters. Both white and black southerners accepted Jesus as their savior, took the Bible as the basic text of their religion, and believed in the power of prayer. Both held services that featured the singing of religious songs; both listened as preachers interpreted biblical passages and explained the tenets of the Christian faith. These and other broad similarities reflected the fact that the slaves had adopted the religion of their masters.

"Let My People Go"

But in other ways, the slaves' practice of Christianity did not at all match that of white southerners. The slaves' worship services represented one obvious difference. The religious services of the

Slaves worship at a service held in a cabin. The religious services of slaves were typically more animated than those of their masters.

slaves were usually much more animated and energetic than those of the slaveholders. Hand clapping, dancing, and a call-and-response form of worship—all widespread religious traditions in Africa—were common in services led and attended by slaves during the plantation era. To the slaveholders, who held somewhat more restrained religious services, the worship of the slaves was charged with a level of emotion both alien and deeply intriguing. "The Negroes sobbed and shouted and swayed backward and forward," wrote a white woman who attended a slave prayer service. "It was a little too exciting for me. I would very much have liked to shout too."[52]

The most important difference between white and black concepts of Christianity, however, was theological. The slaves viewed Christianity in ways that reflected their own circumstances. They were drawn to the stories of Old Testament prophets such as Moses, who led the Hebrew people out of slavery in Egypt. Slaves strongly identified with the ancient Hebrews, who had been held captive against their will, and their music, sermons, and stories reflected that sense of connection. "Go down, Moses," reads the refrain of one spiritual, "Way down in Egypt's land/Tell old Pharaoh/To let my people go."[53]

Slaves and whites perceived the importance of certain biblical texts differently as well. The slaves had little use for admonitions such as that of the apostle Paul in Ephesians 6:5, "Servants, be ye obedient to them that are your masters," though white ministers often preached to them on this text. Instead, slaves focused on passages that offered hope of a brighter tomorrow. They had experienced suffering in a way that few whites ever did, and they held tightly to promises of heaven. To them, the expectation of deliverance, whether on earth or after death, was fundamental to their religious beliefs. "Does I believe in 'ligion?" asked one ex-slave. "What else good for colored folks? I ask you if dere ain't a heaven, what's colored folks got to look forward to?"[54]

The desire for a better future could also lead to divergent images of God and Jesus. While some white southerners of the plantation era perceived a direct and vital connection between themselves and God, historians and theologians have noted that many slaveholders viewed God as distant, severe, and patriarchal. To the slaves, in contrast, God and Jesus were both much more

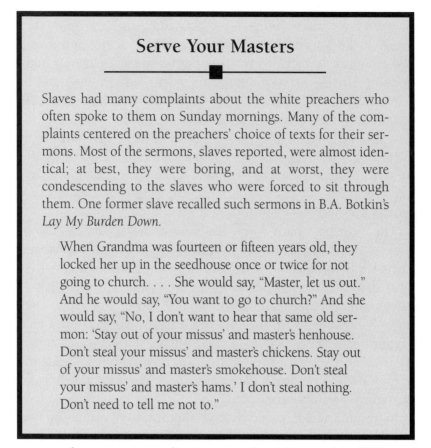

Serve Your Masters

Slaves had many complaints about the white preachers who often spoke to them on Sunday mornings. Many of the complaints centered on the preachers' choice of texts for their sermons. Most of the sermons, slaves reported, were almost identical; at best, they were boring, and at worst, they were condescending to the slaves who were forced to sit through them. One former slave recalled such sermons in B.A. Botkin's *Lay My Burden Down.*

> When Grandma was fourteen or fifteen years old, they locked her up in the seedhouse once or twice for not going to church. . . . She would say, "Master, let us out." And he would say, "You want to go to church?" And she would say, "No, I don't want to hear that same old sermon: 'Stay out of your missus' and master's henhouse. Don't steal your missus' and master's chickens. Stay out of your missus' and master's smokehouse. Don't steal your missus' and master's hams.' I don't steal nothing. Don't need to tell me not to."

commonly seen as immediate, personal, and accessible. This perception helped many slaves survive the burdens of slavery. In a world where a master could beat a slave to death or separate a slave family at whim, an understanding, responsive God could offer hope. "I tells 'em, iffen they keeps praying," remarked one slave preacher, "the Lord will set 'em free."[55]

"A Deep Sympathy of Feeling"

As vibrant and vital as this new culture was, it could not have reached its full flowering without the rise of the plantation system. The colonial era had scattered slaves, isolating them and preventing the flow of exchange that creates and refines a culture. But plantation slavery did the opposite. It brought dozens, sometimes hundreds, of blacks closely together; it had them working the same hours, performing the same tasks, and sharing the same living space. This togetherness helped the slaves form what had been lacking in the colonial era: a sense of community. As one observer noted, "Between slaves on the same plantation there is a deep sympathy of feeling which binds them . . . closely together."[56]

With the help of this community, the new culture flourished. Plantation slaves, unlike their colonial counterparts, did not need to rely on masters and other whites as their main source of new values, ways, and beliefs. Instead, they came to rely on each other. On the typical southern plantation, slaves shared songs and stories, experimented with hairstyles and basketry techniques, and discussed ways of raising children and making gardens grow. Little by little, the individual experiences of these slaves began to coalesce, and a clear and vibrant African American culture took shape.

The migrations of southerners during the plantation era helped foster this new culture, too. Planters needed slaves for their new holdings in Alabama, Texas, or Tennessee. Accordingly, a steady stream of men, women, and children left the older slave states and headed south and west. The moves were wrenching for the slaves, who were uprooted from their homes and too often forced to leave family members and friends behind. But the effect on the burgeoning African American culture was quite different. The new plantations allowed slaves from different regions to come together and pass on the customs and ways of their people.

By the early 1800s the formation of a single African American culture was well under way. By 1860 that culture had taken root throughout the plantation South. As the years wore on, it became more and more likely that slaves, no matter where they lived in the region, played the same games, danced the same dances, celebrated the same holidays, and worshipped in the same ways. No serious historian, of course, sees the rise of this rich new culture as adequate recompense for centuries of bondage. Still, it is one of the great ironies of slavery that the development of this rich and distinctive slave culture was sparked, encouraged, and in a sense made possible by the rise of the brutal and exploitative plantation system.

Chapter Six

The Politics of Slavery

Although the burdens and tragedies of American slavery fell almost exclusively on the slaves themselves, the effects of the institution were much broader than that. By the early nineteenth century, slavery was the foundation of the southern economy. Most of the region's wealth was attributable, either directly or indirectly, to the sale of agricultural products grown and harvested by slave workers. In such an economy, there was little incentive to develop manufacturing capabilities. The result was an agrarian lifestyle almost entirely dependent on slave labor.

The effects of slavery, however, extended far beyond the borders of the states where it was legal. As the nineteenth century wore on, a small but growing band of northern activists grew concerned about the institution. Their objections to slavery were generally couched in ethical terms: Slavery, they argued, was immoral and wrong. Southerners responded to these attacks by defending their institution. Slavery, they asserted, was ethically acceptable, good for the slave owners and good for the slaves as well.

As the country changed and developed throughout the early 1800s, the intensity of these charges and countercharges increased. More and more issues of American policy seemed tinged by what came to be called the "slave question." By the 1850s the problem of slavery had spun out into a dozen or more interrelated controversies, and was rapidly overshadowing all other issues of American political and civic life. Increasingly, northerners and southerners viewed each other with suspicion and hostility. Because of slavery and the controversies surrounding it, the country was on the verge of disunion.

Far from being a limited phenomenon that affected only the slaves and their masters, then, the institution of slavery came to have a dramatic impact on the American people. The political conflicts over slavery would disrupt the life of the nation and lead

President George Washington looks on as a delegate signs the U.S. Constitution. The issue of slavery was very divisive even at the time the document was drafted.

THE FOUNDATION OF AMERICAN GOVERNMENT

eventually to disunion, violence, and war. In this way, the institution of slavery would have a direct effect on nearly every man, woman, and child in the United States.

Early Conflicts

American conflicts over slavery date back to the formation of the country. Even during the writing of the U.S. Constitution, the issue of slavery proved divisive. The slave trade was one example. At the Constitutional Convention held in Philadelphia in 1787, many delegates from northern states argued that the slave trade was a relic of a less enlightened time. Reasoning that the slave population would continue to grow as slaves had children, some of these men proposed an immediate ban on the importation of slaves. Representatives of several southern states, however, objected. After some debate, the two sides compromised. The slave trade was to remain legal for twenty years, and then would be banned forever.

The writers of the Constitution compromised on slavery in other ways as well. Since states with larger populations would receive more seats in the House of Representatives, southerners wanted to count slaves as free people for this purpose of determining representation. Northerners, however, disagreed. They pointed out that slaves were treated as property, not as human beings. Since northern horses and cattle did not count toward representation, argued one New England politician, "why should . . . representation be increased to the southward on account of the number of slaves?"[57] In the end, delegates compromised again and agreed to count each slave as three-fifths of a person.

Two other issues arose during this period as well, although at the time neither seemed particularly controversial. The first involved fugitive slaves. Southerners insisted that runaway slaves should remain the property of their owners, no matter how much time had elapsed since their escape. If the fugitives were recaptured, southerners argued, whoever found them should return them to their rightful owners. Only a few northerners objected, so a provision to that effect was included in the Constitution.

The second issue involved slavery in territories that might be claimed by the United States in the future. Some of the founders argued that slavery, for moral reasons, should be prohibited in

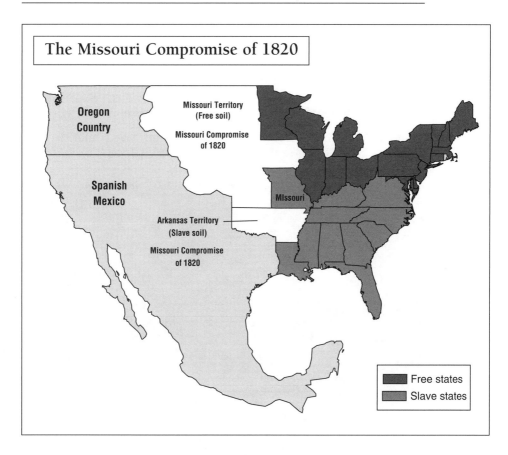

The Missouri Compromise of 1820

Oregon Country

Missouri Territory (Free soil)
Missouri Compromise of 1820

Spanish Mexico

Missouri

Arkansas Territory (Slave soil)
Missouri Compromise of 1820

Free states
Slave states

any new territory. But others were not so sure. Instead of establishing a firm policy, then, the two sides compromised. In 1787, in a measure that was not incorporated into the Constitution, the government banned slavery in the new Northwest Territory, the present-day states of Ohio, Indiana, Illinois, Michigan, and Wisconsin, along with northeastern Minnesota. At the same time, southerners were permitted to bring their slaves into Kentucky, Tennessee, and other territories farther to the south.

The Missouri Compromise

On the one hand, these compromises were necessary to assure the survival of the new nation. Knowing that the issue of slavery had the potential to pull the nation apart, the founders agreed to lay their differences aside. But the decision to compromise had a cost. In sidestepping the disagreements over slavery, the founders gave up an opportunity to resolve the problem before it became an all-consuming issue. In the end, nothing had been solved; the issue had simply been deferred to another generation.

Within a few dozen years, the price of the founders' decision was apparent. It was clear by the early 1800s that the economic and political interests of North and South were diverging—and

Publisher William Lloyd Garrison (left) and freed slave Frederick Douglass (right) used Garrison's antislavery newspaper, the *Liberator*, to promote their abolitionist ideology.

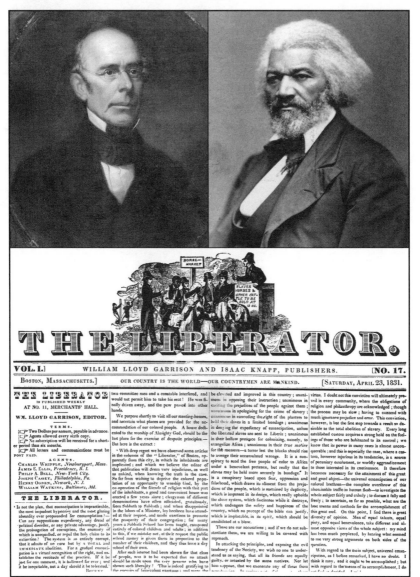

that the basic reason for the split was slavery. The South maintained and championed the institution; the North did not. The combination made for a volatile and unstable political environment. By the second decade of the new century, American political leaders were well aware that the sectional differences might escalate into full-scale conflict.

But like their predecessors, the leaders of the early 1800s could find no easy way to resolve the situation once and for all. Instead, they emulated the founders and sought to defuse the issue through further compromise. The most important of these arose in 1820, when the slave territory of Missouri applied for statehood. Although Missouri met all the requirements of statehood, no corresponding free territory was populous enough to join the Union at the same time. During the previous few years, states had been added to the Union in pairs in an attempt to keep North and South carefully balanced, with neither side holding an advantage in the Senate. The admission of Missouri, though, would cause the slave states to outnumber the free states. Northerners howled in protest; southerners blithely continued with plans to make Missouri a state. Suspicion and hostility reigned, and some leaders feared that violence would break out over the issue.

Bloodshed was averted in the end, but only barely. Under the so-called Missouri Compromise, Missouri was admitted as a slave state, to be balanced by the admission of Maine, a new free state created from a part of Massachusetts geographically unconnected to the rest of the state. The Missouri Compromise also addressed the question of slavery in territories that had yet to apply for statehood. The plan permanently banned slavery north and west of Missouri, while allowing the institution in the Arkansas Territory to the south. The agreement was acceptable to both sides. But Thomas Jefferson, by now an old man, suspected it would not last. "[The conflict] is hushed, indeed, for the moment," he wrote. "But this is a reprieve only, not a final sentence."[58]

The Abolitionists

During the American nation's first fifty years, the debate over slavery usually touched on practical issues: slavery in the territories, for example, or how best to maintain the balance of power between the free states and the slave states. But in the 1830s the debate took on a moral dimension, and the argument over slavery took on an increasingly strident tone. As a consequence, attitudes on both sides soon began to harden.

Part of the change was due to a group of antislavery northerners known as abolitionists. The abolitionists varied in their approach and their goals, but they shared a desire to eliminate slavery not just in the territories but wherever it existed. They documented the cruelties of slavery and demanded immediate emancipation for all slaves. "The slaveholder," declared Boston minister Amos Phelps, speaking for many, "should cease at once to hold or employ human beings as property."[59]

In making their case against slavery, the abolitionists of the 1830s relied on familiar assertions. Most notably, they appealed to religious morality and natural law. "Is not God a God of justice to *all* his creatures?"[60] asked David Walker, a free black antislavery activist originally from North Carolina. In a similar vein, former slave and abolitionist leader Frederick Douglass highlighted the inconsistencies between the realities of slavery and the pro-liberty messages of Independence Day, a holiday celebrated with great enthusiasm by most white southerners during the plantation era. The contradiction, Douglass pointed out, was glaring; more than that, it made the slave bitterly aware of "the gross injustice and cruelty to which he is the constant victim."[61]

Many abolitionists were less famous for what they said than for how they said it. These activists, including Douglass and Walker as well as preacher Theodore Weld and newspaper editor William Lloyd Garrison, used uncompromising and inflammatory language to make their points. For most, this was a deliberate choice, designed to attract attention and put southerners on the defensive. "I do not wish to think, or speak, or write, with moderation," Garrison explained in the first issue of his antislavery newspaper, the *Liberator*. "I am in earnest—I will not equivocate—I will not excuse—I will not retreat a single inch—AND I WILL BE HEARD."[62]

Southern Intransigence

At the same time that the abolitionists were mounting attacks on slavery, southern planters were modifying their own views

Slavery and the Declaration of Independence

Slavery was a politically charged issue in America even before the writing of the Constitution. One of Thomas Jefferson's early drafts of the Declaration of Independence, for instance, made a pointed reference to the slave trade and the role played by the British in establishing it. "He [that is, Britain's King George III] has waged cruel war against human nature itself," Jefferson charged (as quoted in Don Fehrenbacher's *The Slaveholding Republic*), "violating its most sacred rights of life and liberty in the persons of a distant people who never offended him, capturing & carrying them into slavery in another hemisphere."

The statement matched the general tenor of the declaration, which enumerated the ways in which the king interfered with the colonists' rights and freedoms. But the reference did not appear in the final document. The exact reasons for the deletion are unclear today. Many historians believe, however, that leaders from Deep South colonies such as Georgia and South Carolina were uncomfortable with the tone of Jefferson's language. To say that the slaves enjoyed "sacred rights of . . . liberty," as Jefferson had put it, raised the obvious question of why the slaves were not free. Thus, the slaveholders of the Deep South urged the removal of the offending clause. Eager to present a united front against the common British enemy, Jefferson and his supporters agreed to delete it.

on the institution. Once, slavery had been perceived, even by many southerners, as a necessary evil. Men like Jefferson had been embarrassed by its presence in a supposedly civilized society. By 1830, however, southerners no longer apologized for their peculiar institution. Instead, southern whites were increasingly adopting the notion that slavery was a positive good. As George Fitzhugh put it, "Domestic slavery is right in principle and practice."[63]

These advocates of slavery, sometimes known as the fire-eaters, asserted that the slave system represented the best of all possible worlds. Slavery, they argued, protected and defended blacks, whose inferior intelligence was taken for granted by near-ly all white southerners. Cruelty toward slaves, these advocates claimed, was rare. Escape attempts were rarer still. Indeed, many southerners asserted, the slaves had no wish for freedom. "Our slaves," argued South Carolina governor George McDuffie, "are cheerful, contented, and happy, much beyond the general condi-tion of the human race."[64]

By the early 1830s, the abolitionists and the fire-eaters were waging a bitter battle of words. Sometimes, the arguments were rational and measured. More often, they were neither. Proslavery activists charged that the abolitionists encouraged slaves to take up arms against their masters; abolitionists characterized slave owners as evil men who made covenants with the devil. Slave-holders claimed that black slaves were better off than free white laborers in the North; abolitionists insisted that the slaveholders were destroying fundamental American principles. A southern politician called abolitionists "unrestrained fanatics."[65] William Lloyd Garrison referred to slaveholders as "treasonable disunion-ists."[66]

Reasoned or not, the charges of the abolitionists did have a sig-nificant, and perhaps unintended, effect: They pushed the South toward unanimity on the slave question. For years, southerners had held and expressed varying opinions on slavery. But by the early 1830s virtually the entire South had adopted the enthusias-tically proslavery view of men like McDuffie. As slaveholders rushed to champion their institution, they suppressed honest debate on the subject. Now, white southerners no longer ques-tioned any aspect of slavery, at least not in public. One Georgia man was tarred, feathered, and set on fire for subscribing to William Lloyd Garrison's newspaper. A Virginia man was whipped for saying that "black men have, in the abstract, a right to their freedom."[67]

The effect of the abolitionists on the North, in contrast, was much more muted. At first, the words of leaders such as Garrison and Weld did little to incite northern opinion against slavery. Though the majority of northerners opposed slavery in the abstract, their opposition did not run very deep. Hardly any northerners considered blacks—slave or free—to be their equals.

Nor did most northern citizens think it their business to tell the southern states how to run their affairs. Well into the 1840s, then, the abolitionists were lonely voices, a band of activists from a largely apathetic North heaping scorn upon an increasingly unified and angry South.

Slavery and the Territories

But in the late 1840s northern apathy began to change. The immediate reason was a question about the status of a wide swath of land that ran from the Rocky Mountains west to California. This land, known as the Mexican Cession, had been acquired by the United States in 1848 following a war with Mexico. Since it represented a new addition to the country, the Mexican Cession was not covered under the terms of the Missouri Compromise. Leaders from the North and the South immediately set to work determining whether slavery should be permitted in this new land.

To southerners, the answer to this question was obvious. Southern soldiers had helped win the war with Mexico; southerners, therefore, should share in the fruits of their victory. The fire-eaters demanded that the new territory be opened to slavery. Most northerners, meanwhile, even if they did not accept the abolitionists' argument that slavery should be abolished where it already

Illinois senator Stephen A. Douglas suggested that Congress repeal the Missouri Compromise.

87

existed, had no desire to let the institution expand any farther. The passions of the moment swept up even moderate thinkers on both sides, and northerners and southerners accused each other of trying to run the country.

Disaster was finally averted by yet another compromise, this one called the Compromise of 1850. As part of this deal, the government banned slavery in California, which had been settled mainly by northerners, and postponed a decision on the legality of slavery elsewhere in the new territory. For many northerners, the Compromise of 1850 did not do enough to check the spread of slavery. For many in the South, however, it did entirely too much. Though the measure eventually passed, its fate was in doubt until the very end, and the bitterness of the debate revealed just how separated North and South had become.

But not even this latest compromise could put to rest the question of slavery in the territories. In 1854 the issue arose yet again. According to the Missouri Compromise, slavery had been forbidden in the Great Plains territories west and north of Missouri. Now, however, southern slaveholders were intent on removing that barrier. With their encouragement, Illinois politician Stephen A. Douglas proposed a bill called the Kansas-Nebraska Act. Under this plan, the Missouri Compromise would be repealed and replaced with a new model that would allow the people of newly organized Plains territories to choose whether or not to allow slavery.

To southerners, the Kansas-Nebraska Act seemed perfectly reasonable. To many northerners, however, the act was an outrage. Staunch abolitionists were particularly upset, but even less radical northerners found the bill impossible to accept. In their opinion, changing the rules to open these free territories to slavery was unforgivable—and set an extremely dangerous precedent. If free territories could be opened to slaveholders, northerners worried, what was to prevent southerners from demanding that slavery be legalized in, say, Ohio or Vermont?

The Split Widens

Despite bitter opposition to the Kansas-Nebraska Act through much of the North, Douglas and a few other northern legislators supported it. The bill passed. Three years later, in a case involv-

John Brown's Raid

---◼---

In 1859 a northern abolitionist named John Brown gathered together a small band of followers and staged a raid on the U.S. arsenal in the town of Harpers Ferry, now in West Virginia. His intention was to arm the slaves in the immediate area and begin a general rebellion among the slaves of the South. The raid took the community and the government completely by surprise, and Brown managed to seize a few weapons and hostages for a time. However, Brown's plans had no real chance of succeeding. He was soon overpowered, arrested, and convicted of treason. Two months later, he was hanged.

The raid was widely condemned by northerners and southerners alike. Even some of the North's most rabid antislavery activists were deeply troubled by Brown's use of violence. Nevertheless, southerners drew a clear connection between the words of the abolitionists and the deeds of John Brown. In their eyes, rebellion was what the abolitionists had wanted all along, the pacifist statements of abolitionist leaders such as William Lloyd Garrison notwithstanding. The raid thus served to confirm southerners' worst fears about the North, and pushed the country closer to disunion.

ing a slave named Dred Scott, the Supreme Court went even further: It ruled that Congress had no power to forbid slavery in any territories. While southerners applauded the decision, northerners bitterly objected. The abolitionists had once stood almost alone in their condemnation of slavery and the South. Now, when Garrison charged that the South was trying to make the North "cower and obey like a plantation slave,"[68] northerners listened—and voiced their agreement.

The question of slavery in the territories was not the only way in which slavery split the two regions. The handling of runaway slaves was another. As part of the Compromise of 1850, Congress had passed a bill known as the Fugitive Slave Act. Under this act, the government lifted most legal protections previously offered to suspected runaways captured in the North. In addition, it obligated

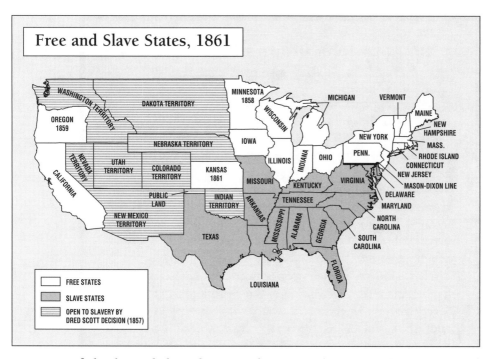

Free and Slave States, 1861

WASHINGTON TERRITORY
OREGON 1859
DAKOTA TERRITORY
MINNESOTA 1858
MICHIGAN
VERMONT
MAINE
NEW HAMPSHIRE
NEVADA TERRITORY
UTAH TERRITORY
NEBRASKA TERRITORY
IOWA
WISCONSIN
NEW YORK
MASS.
RHODE ISLAND
CONNECTICUT
CALIFORNIA
COLORADO TERRITORY
KANSAS 1861
ILLINOIS
INDIANA
OHIO
PENN.
NEW JERSEY
MASON-DIXON LINE
PUBLIC LAND
INDIAN TERRITORY
MISSOURI
KENTUCKY
VIRGINIA
DELAWARE
MARYLAND
NEW MEXICO TERRITORY
ARKANSAS
TENNESSEE
NORTH CAROLINA
TEXAS
MISSISSIPPI
ALABAMA
GEORGIA
SOUTH CAROLINA
LOUISIANA
FLORIDA

☐ FREE STATES
▨ SLAVE STATES
▤ OPEN TO SLAVERY BY DRED SCOTT DECISION (1857)

federal marshals and even ordinary northerners to help catch and return fugitive slaves. The South viewed the new law as a test of northern commitment to the Union. "The continued existence of the United States as one nation," editorialized one southern newspaper, "depends upon the full and faithful execution of the Fugitive Slave Bill."[69]

But northerners had other ideas. Even moderates, who were inclined to allow slavery where it already existed, denounced the law as unfair, unjust, and downright wrong. They saw it as another attempt by southerners to force slavery down their throats. In response, several states passed laws to nullify the Fugitive Slave Act within their borders, a legally dubious move but one that expressed northern anger. One northerner noted that the people of his Michigan county had paid little attention to slavery until the passage of the act. "It is greatly changed since," he wrote. "Our citizens side almost with entire unanimity with the poor captives and fugitives, and there is deep feeling on the subject."[70]

By 1860 the split between the regions had widened into an enormous gap. Moderates on both sides had virtually disappeared. The people of the North complained that the country was being run by a group of powerful slaveholders eager to expand their empire across the continent. The people of the South, in turn, complained that the North was trying to stamp out their way of life. Churches split into northern and southern branches. Businesses cut ties with customers in the other region. Talk of secession, present in some southern circles for several years, became louder and more immediate. Angry and ready for a fight, the two regions faced each other, literally and figuratively, across the Mason-Dixon Line.

The wedge that had split the country, far more than any other, was slavery. Slavery had bedeviled the founders of the nation, and had done the same for every succeeding generation of Americans. Through an initial compromise, the Union had been established as a place half-slave and half-free, a balance that continued with further compromise. But the issue of slavery had finally grown too weighty, too personal, and too intense. Almost seventy-five years after the ratification of the Constitution, the burden of slavery was about to break the Union completely in two.

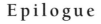

The End of Slavery

The presidential campaign of 1860 was waged by four major candidates who represented a wide variety of political perspectives. Two of the candidates—John Bell of Tennessee and Stephen A. Douglas, the Illinois legislator who had worked with slaveholders to pass the Missouri Compromise—were perceived as moderates, and they fared the worst. Bell, who campaigned on a platform of national unity, carried three states of the Upper South but made little impression elsewhere. Douglas, in turn, drew many more popular votes than Bell but did even worse in the Electoral College. Though Douglas had significant support in many northern states and parts of the Upper South, he won just twelve electoral votes.

The mass of public opinion, instead, was drawn to the two candidates perceived to be the most extreme. John C. Breckinridge of Kentucky was the southern half of this equation. A slaveholder himself, Breckinridge staunchly supported the rights—and the demands—of southern whites. Breckinridge's appeal was limited to the South; every electoral vote he earned, and most of the popular votes as well, came from slave states. In the end, he carried most of his region and came away from the election with seventy-two electoral votes.

It was not enough, however. Breckinridge's vote totals did not come close to those of the fourth candidate, Abraham Lincoln. Another Illinois politician with a history of opposing the spread of slavery to the territories, Lincoln was in a sense the mirror image of Breckinridge. Where Breckinridge did not win a single northern electoral vote, Lincoln did not even appear on the ballot in many southern states. Still, the votes of the North were enough to give Lincoln the election. Although he won only about four of every ten votes cast—and virtually none outside the free states—his 180 electoral votes were enough to sweep him past his opponents and into office.

Lincoln's election had an immediate impact on the states of the South. Lincoln, no admirer of slavery, had come to prominence as a member of the Republican Party. This political party had been formed only a few years earlier on a promise to keep slavery out of the territories. Lincoln was not an abolitionist: As he repeated many times before and immediately after the election, he had no intention of interfering with slavery where it already existed. Still, many slaveholders, citing Lincoln's position on slavery in the West, doubted his sincerity. As one southern newspaper editorialized, the election of Lincoln was a "deliberate, cold-blooded insult and outrage on the people of the slaveholding states."[71]

In the poisoned atmosphere of the time, the result was predictable. One by one, a succession of southern states seceded from the Union and set up a new nation of their own: the Confederate States of America. For the residents of these states, preserving slavery was more important than preserving the Union. Lincoln, however, took the opposite position. In his opinion, the Confederate states had no right to secede, and the Union should be paramount. When South Carolina demanded that Union forces evacuate Fort Sumter in the Charleston harbor, Lincoln refused. And when southerners fired on the fort, Lincoln put out a call for volunteers. The Civil War had begun.

Slavery and the War

At first, Lincoln portrayed the war simply as a battle to preserve the Union, not an attempt to eliminate slavery throughout the South. That was a viewpoint entirely consistent with the comments he had made earlier. And for the first eighteen months or

When Abraham Lincoln won the presidency in 1860, Southern states began to secede from the Union to form their own nation: the Confederate States of America.

so of the conflict, Lincoln stuck to this position. Saving the Union, he said again and again, was what counted. Freeing the slaves was important only if it helped fulfill the greater goal. "If I could save the Union without freeing *any* slave," he explained in a summation of his principles, "I would do it; and if I could save it by freeing *all* the slaves, I would do it; and if I could do it by freeing some and leaving others alone, I would also do that."[72]

There were good political reasons for Lincoln's refusal to frame the war as a conflict over slavery. Not all Northerners were abolitionists, after all. And even those who opposed the institution were not necessarily ready to fight to eliminate it. In particular, four slave states of the Upper South had opted to stay with the Union rather than secede, and Lincoln was very eager to keep these states in the Union camp. Thus, he took great care not to offend those Unionists who had no particular quarrel with slavery.

But as the war continued, abolitionist Northerners increasingly urged Lincoln to take a moral stand against slavery. They argued that launching an attack on slavery, though potentially upsetting Unionists from the border states, would reinvigorate the cause and win the support of antislavery activists. They also pointed to more practical concerns. There were rumors, for example, that England or France might enter the war on the Confederate side. Both countries had economic ties to the South, and both had quarreled with the North. But neither country had any love for slavery. If Lincoln could redefine the war as an honorable crusade against human bondage, not as the violent suppression of a revolt, then England and France would probably stay out of the conflict.

Lincoln was soon persuaded by these arguments. In September 1862 he issued a document called the Emancipation Proclamation. This edict announced that all slaves living in the Confederacy as of January 1, 1863, would be "then, thenceforward, and forever free."[73] The document was bold and far reaching, but it did not actually free a single slave. Lincoln had made sure not to insult his supporters in the slaveholding states still loyal to the Union. The document did not apply to those states, or to Confederate territory captured by Union troops. It affected only the Confederacy itself, and of course Lincoln had no means of enforcing his edict there. The Emancipation Proclamation's importance, then, was not in what it said but in what it represented.

And what it represented made an enormous difference in how the war was fought and how it was perceived. No longer was the North fighting simply to restore the Union. Instead, it was battling for a broader, more principled cause: a struggle against the great evil of slavery. In January 1863 the ultimate outcome of the war was still impossible to predict. But by issuing the Emancipation Proclamation, Lincoln had made one point abundantly clear.

If and when the North won, it was absolutely certain that slavery would be abolished.

The Contrabands

In fact, in some parts of the South, slavery was slowly being abolished even before the Emancipation Proclamation was drafted. This emancipation, however, had nothing to do with governmental edicts; instead, it was carried out by the slaves themselves. Wherever Union armies pushed into the Confederacy, slaves began slipping away from their plantations and hurrying to the safety of Union lines. "I make up my mind to go," remembered a former slave who realized that Union troops were nearby, "and I leaves with de chunk of meat and cornbread and am on my way, half skeert to death."[74]

Confederate officials demanded that Union officers return the runaways, known to the Northern troops as "contrabands," but the requests were generally refused. There was a clear military value to keeping the runaways: Every escaped slave meant one fewer field hand to provide the Confederacy with cloth, wheat, or corn. And each new contraband could be put to use helping the Union's war effort, whether by building forts, cooking for the troops, or becoming soldiers themselves. Refusing to send back the runaways thus dealt a double blow to the Confederacy.

In theory, the Union government could have kept these slaves as slaves, even without returning them to their former owners. But in practice, that was never an option. It would have been hypocritical for the North, free of slavery for so many years, to link itself with slavery once again. Nor would such a move have been politically wise, given the anger against the slaveholding Confederacy that prevailed in the North and the intense Northern opposition to the Fugitive Slave Act. So Union officials did the only thing they could: They granted the contrabands their freedom.

As the war went on, more and more slaves availed themselves of the opportunity to flee to Union lines. Each new contraband was a blow to the slave system and to the Confederacy. Union officials were delighted. They had ordered their soldiers to interfere with the Confederate war effort in any way possible. Freeing the slaves, it turned out, was one of the most effective ways of accomplishing

Slaves like these who escaped behind Union lines during the war were called contrabands. After they arrived in Union territory, they were immediately granted their freedom.

this goal. "To save the Union," sums up historian Bruce Catton, "the North had to destroy the Confederacy, and to destroy the Confederacy it had to destroy slavery."[75] Even before the Emancipation Proclamation, then, slavery was dead, assuming, that is, that the Union won.

Aftermath

And in the end, it did. After four full years, the Civil War came to a close with the surrender of Confederate general Robert E. Lee to the Union's Ulysses S. Grant at Appomattox Courthouse, Virginia, in April 1865. The Union had finally been restored. That December, slavery was formally abolished across the entire country with the passage of the Thirteenth Amendment to the U.S. Constitution. "Neither slavery nor involuntary servitude," the amendment declared, "shall exist within the United States, or any place subject to their jurisdiction."[76] Throughout the South, border states and Confederacy alike, slaves were set free. They were no longer property. Instead, they were fully persons at last.

Thus did slavery die. For years the institution had taken center stage in the life of the American nation. It had created an economy; it had pulled the nation apart; it had divided the people of the country as no issue before or since. Most of all, it had brought devastation and tragedy to the lives of the slaves. The brutality and violence of slavery turned the hearts of many northerners against it, and the abolitionists' charges that the system was immoral and unjust disturbed many more. But the blow that

Congressmen cheer as the House of Representatives passes the Thirteenth Amendment to the Constitution abolishing slavery in December 1865.

> ## "I Takes the Freedom"
>
> ———■———
>
> During the 1930s, nearly seventy years after the end of slavery, interviewers for a government agency tracked down many elderly ex-slaves around the country and asked them to talk about their experiences in slavery. Despite their advanced age, many of these respondents described their early lives in great detail and with great feeling. "They was things past telling," Mary Reynolds recalled, quoted in B.A. Botkin's *Lay My Burden Down*, "but I got the scars on my old body to show to this day." "I never seen nothing but work and tribulations," Katie Rowe remembered. Squires Jackson summed up his experience this way: "Even the best masters in slavery couldn't be as good as the worst person in freedom." When asked which he preferred, slavery or freedom, Henry Banner spoke for nearly all former slaves: "What I likes best, to be slave or free? Well, it's this way. In slavery I owns nothing and never owns nothing. In freedom I's own the home and raise the family. All that cause me worriment, and in slavery I has no worriment, but I takes the freedom."

ended slavery was neither of these things. What brought down the institution, instead, was slavery's own power. The growing influence of the slave South eventually led to regional hostility, secession, and war, a war that the slave system had begun and that would end, at last, in the death of the institution altogether.

Notes

Chapter 1:
The Beginnings of Slavery

1. Quoted in Donald R. Wright, *African Americans in the Colonial Era.* Arlington Heights, IL: Harlan Davidson, 1990, p. 19.
2. Quoted in Charles Johnson and Patricia Smith, *Africans in America: America's Journey Through Slavery.* New York: Harcourt Brace, 1998, p. 38.
3. Quoted in James Oliver Horton and Lois E. Horton, *Hard Road to Freedom: The Story of African America.* New Brunswick, NJ: Rutgers University Press, 2001, p. 29.
4. Quoted in Kenneth Stampp, *The Peculiar Institution.* New York: Knopf, 1967, p. 18.
5. Quoted in Timothy Severin, *The African Adventure.* New York: Dutton, 1973, p. 63.
6. Quoted in Basil Davidson, *The African Slave Trade.* Boston: Little, Brown, 1961, p. 89.
7. Quoted in Johnson and Smith, *Africans in America*, p. 68.
8. Quoted in Horton and Horton, *Hard Road to Freedom*, p. 18.
9. John Hope Franklin and Alfred A. Moss Jr., *From Slavery to Freedom*, 8th ed. New York: Knopf, 2000, p. 44.
10. Quoted in Johnson and Smith, *Africans in America*, p. 72.
11. Quoted in Johnson and Smith, *Africans in America*, p. 74.
12. Quoted in Horton and Horton, *Hard Road to Freedom*, p. 31.

Chapter 2:
The Rise of the Plantation South

13. Quoted in William Dudley, ed., *Slavery: Opposing Viewpoints.* San Diego: Greenhaven, 1992, p. 28.
14. Quoted in Dudley, *Slavery*, p. 41.
15. Franklin and Moss, *From Slavery to Freedom*, p. 66.
16. Quoted in Johnson and Smith, *Africans in America*, p. 203.
17. Quoted in Harvey Wish, ed., *Slavery in the South.* New York: Noonday, 1964, p. 232.
18. Quoted in Johnson and Smith, *Africans in America*, p. 268.
19. Quoted in Stampp, *The Peculiar Institution*, p. 27.
20. Quoted in Stampp, *The Peculiar Institution*, p. 39.
21. Quoted in Stampp, *The Peculiar Institution*, p. 43.

Chapter 3:
The Experience of Slavery

22. Quoted in Wish, *Slavery in the South*, p. 77.
23. Quoted in Stanley Feldstein, *Once a*

Slave: The Slave's View of Slavery. New York: William Morrow, 1971, p. 47.

24. Quoted in August Meier and Elliott Rudwick, eds., *The Making of Black America*, vol. 1. New York: Atheneum, 1969, p. 149.

25. Quoted in B.A. Botkin, *Lay My Burden Down.* Chicago: University of Chicago Press, 1945, p. 166.

26. Quoted in Eugene Genovese, *Roll, Jordan, Roll: The World the Slaves Made.* New York: Vintage, 1972, p. 66.

27. Quoted in Charles L. Blockson, *The Underground Railroad.* New York: Prentice-Hall, 1987, pp. 16–17.

28. Quoted in Franklin and Moss, *From Slavery to Freedom*, p. 160.

29. Quoted in Genovese, *Roll, Jordan, Roll*, p. 66.

30. Quoted in Botkin, *Lay My Burden Down*, p. 170.

31. George Fitzhugh, *Sociology for the South, or the Failure of Free Society.* Richmond, VA: A. Morris, 1854, p. 246.

32. Quoted in Dudley, *Slavery*, p. 102.

33. Quoted in Blockson, *The Underground Railroad*, p. 65.

34. Quoted in Botkin, *Lay My Burden Down*, p. 120.

35. Quoted in Stampp, *The Peculiar Institution*, p. 294.

36. Quoted in Wish, *Slavery in the South*, p. 270.

37. Quoted in Blockson, *The Underground Railroad*, p. 89.

Chapter 4: Challenges from Within

38. Quoted in Genovese, *Roll, Jordan, Roll*, p. 300.

39. Quoted in Stampp, *The Peculiar Institution*, p. 116.

40. Quoted in Earl Conrad, *Harriet Tubman.* New York: Paul S. Eriksson, 1943, p. 36.

41. Quoted in Gilbert Osofsky, ed., *Puttin' On Ole Massa.* New York: Harper and Row, 1969, p. 205.

42. Quoted in Wish, *Slavery in the South*, p. 118.

43. Quoted in Botkin, *Lay My Burden Down*, p. 175.

44. Quoted in Stampp, *The Peculiar Institution*, p. 138.

45. Quoted in Robin D.G. Kelley and Earl Lewis, eds., *To Make Our World Anew: A History of African Americans.* New York: Oxford University Press, 2000, p. 198.

Chapter 5: Creating a Culture

46. Quoted in Genovese, *Roll, Jordan, Roll*, p. 249.

47. Quoted in William F. Allen et al., *Slave Songs of the United States.* New York: A. Simpson, 1867, p. vi.

48. Quoted in Kelley and Lewis, *To Make Our World Anew*, p. 86.

49. Nathan Irvin Huggins, *Black Odyssey: The Afro-American Ordeal in Slavery.* New York: Vintage, 1977, p. 81.

50. Quoted in Julius Lester, *To Be a Slave.* New York: Dial, 1968, p. 103.

51. Quoted in Botkin, *Lay My Burden Down*, p. 160.
52. Quoted in Genovese, *Roll, Jordan, Roll*, p. 267.
53. Quoted in John A. Lomax and Alan Lomax, *Best Loved American Folk Songs.* New York: Grosset and Dunlap, 1947, p. 373.
54. Quoted in Genovese, *Roll, Jordan, Roll*, p. 251.
55. Quoted in Botkin, *Lay My Burden Down*, p. 26.
56. Quoted in Genovese, *Roll, Jordan, Roll*, p. 622.

Chapter 6:
The Politics of Slavery

57. Quoted in Kelley and Lewis, *To Make Our World Anew*, p. 135.
58. Quoted in Allan Nevins and Henry Steele Commager, *A Pocket History of the United States*, 6th ed. New York: Pocket, 1976, p. 162.
59. Quoted in Dudley, *Slavery*, p. 179.
60. Quoted in Franklin and Moss, *From Slavery to Freedom*, p. 196.
61. Quoted in Kelley and Lewis, *To Make Our World Anew*, p. 211.
62. Quoted in Henry Mayer, *All on Fire: William Lloyd Garrison and the Abolition of Slavery.* New York: St. Martin's, 1998, p. 112.
63. Quoted in Wish, *Slavery in the South*, p. 277.
64. Quoted in Dudley, *Slavery*, p. 69.
65. Quoted in Russel B. Nye, *William Lloyd Garrison and the Humanitarian Reformers.* Boston: Little, Brown, 1995, p. 52.
66. Quoted in Dudley, *Slavery*, p. 159.
67. Quoted in Franklin and Moss, *From Slavery to Freedom*, p. 213.
68. Quoted in Mayer, *All on Fire*, p. 439.
69. Quoted in Don E. Fehrenbacher, *The Slaveholding Republic.* New York: Oxford University Press, 2001, p. 233.
70. Quoted in Nye, *William Lloyd Garrison and the Humanitarian Reformers*, p. 158.

Epilogue: The End of Slavery

71. Quoted in Fehrenbacher, *The Slaveholding Republic*, p. 295.
72. Quoted in Dudley, *Slavery*, p. 266.
73. Quoted in Avalon Project at Yale Law School, *Documents on Slavery*, www.yale.edu/lawweb/avalon/slavery.htm.
74. Quoted in Ira Berlin, Marc Favreau, and Steven F. Miller, *Remembering Slavery.* New York: New Press, 1998, p. 219.
75. Bruce Catton, *The Civil War.* Boston: Houghton Mifflin, 1960, p. 174.
76. U.S. Constitution, Amendment XIII.

For Further Reading

Gary Barr, *Slavery in the United States*. Chicago: Heinemann Library, 2004. A general history of the institution. Covers such topics as the abolitionists, the creation of slave communities, and the origins of the slave trade.

David Boyle, *African Americans*. Hauppauge, NY: Barron's, 2003. A survey of African American history, with particular emphasis on the period of slavery and the plantation South.

Tonya Buell, *Slavery in America: A Primary Source History of the Intolerable Practice of Slavery*. New York: Rosen, 2004. An emphasis on primary-source materials. Provides copies of documents and artifacts such as antislavery newspaper pages and slave passes.

Stephen Currie, *Life of a Slave on a Southern Plantation*. San Diego: Lucent, 2000. This book focuses on the daily lives of the slaves who worked on southern plantations during the early 1800s. Includes many direct quotations from slaves.

———, *Slavery: Opposing Viewpoints Digests*. San Diego: Greenhaven, 1999. A detailed explanation of the historical arguments made both in support of slavery and in opposition to it. Includes a documents section as well.

Judith Edwards, *Abolitionists and Slave Resistance: Breaking the Chains of Slavery*. Berkeley Heights, NJ: Enslow, 2004. Rebellions, runaways, and the impact of the antislavery movement in the United States.

Paul Erickson, *Daily Life on a Southern Plantation 1853*. London: Breslich and Foss, 1997. A picture book reconstructing what life might have been like on a Louisiana plantation shortly before the Civil War.

Alice Mulcahey Fleming, *Frederick Douglass: From Slave to Statesman*. New York: Power Plus, 2004. A biography of the famous slave-turned-abolitionist.

Meg Greene, *Slave Young, Slave Long: The American Slave Experience*. Minneapolis: Lerner, 1999. A well-illustrated, attractive volume describing slavery; emphasizes the slave's point of view.

Julius Lester, *To Be a Slave*. New York: Dial, 1968. A short but valuable book made up mainly of direct quotations from slaves, along with commentary. One of the first books to present a slave's view of slavery.

Patricia McKissack and Fredrick L. McKissack, *Days of Jubilee: The End of Slavery in the United States*. New York: Scholastic, 2003. Chronicles the steps that led to the emancipation of the slaves and the abolition of American slavery.

————, *Rebels Against Slavery: American Slave Revolts.* New York: Scholastic, 1996. A well-written history of slave rebellions from colonial times through the Civil War.

Tim McNeese, *The Rise and Fall of American Slavery.* Berkeley Heights, NJ: Enslow, 2004. Explores issues such as the slave trade, the rise of King Cotton, and the eventual achievement of emancipation for all the slaves.

Deborah Gray White, *Let My People Go: African Americans 1804–1860.* New York: Oxford University Press, 1996. A readable and useful history of the plantation era with extensive illustrations.

Richard Worth, *The Slave Trade in America: Cruel Commerce.* Berkeley Heights, NJ: Enslow, 2004. A description of the slave trade: how it began, how it worked, and how it affected the lives of the slaves.

Works Consulted

William F. Allen et al., *Slave Songs of the United States*. New York: A. Simpson, 1867. One of the first collections of slave songs, gathered by northerners soon after the close of the Civil War.

Ira Berlin, Marc Favreau, and Steven F. Miller, *Remembering Slavery*. New York: New Press, 1998. Edited excerpts from interviews with former slaves, collected during the 1930s. Includes valuable commentary and background information.

Charles L. Blockson, *The Underground Railroad*. New York: Prentice-Hall, 1987. A useful book about fugitive slaves and their experiences. Includes firsthand accounts, along with analysis and background information.

B.A. Botkin, *Lay My Burden Down*. Chicago: University of Chicago Press, 1945. This book focuses on the 1930s slave narratives, and ranks among the most important primary sources for understanding slavery.

Bruce Catton, *The Civil War.* Boston: Houghton Mifflin, 1960. A well-written, one-volume history of the war by one of America's greatest popular historians.

Earl Conrad, *Harriet Tubman*. New York: Paul S. Eriksson, 1943. An early biography of the famous runaway slave, Underground Railroad conductor, and abolitionist.

Basil Davidson, *The African Slave Trade*. Boston: Little, Brown, 1961. A short but valuable history of the slave trade. Davidson discusses who was brought to the Americas, how the trade was carried out, and what the result of the trade was in the New World as well as in Africa.

William Dudley, ed., *Slavery: Opposing Viewpoints*. San Diego: Greenhaven, 1992. Documents and readings pertaining to American slavery, framed as a series of debates; topics include the treatment of slaves, the morality of slavery, the practicality of immediate abolition, and more.

Don E. Fehrenbacher, *The Slaveholding Republic*. New York: Oxford University Press, 2001. A history of slavery as it affected—and was affected by—the U.S. government. Fehrenbacher argues that U.S. policy was generally friendly to the slaveholders.

Stanley Feldstein, *Once a Slave: The Slave's View of Slavery*. New York: William Morrow, 1971. Another description of slavery from the perspective of the slaves themselves.

George Fitzhugh, *Sociology for the South, or the Failure of Free Society*. Richmond, VA: A. Morris, 1854. Fitzhugh was one of the most prominent southern nationalists. His book presents the arguments for slavery in an unusually clear way.

John Hope Franklin and Alfred A. Moss Jr., *From Slavery to Freedom*. 8th ed. New York: Knopf, 2000. A thorough history of African Americans, including useful information on the slave system and its impact on black history.

Eugene Genovese, *Roll, Jordan, Roll: The World the Slaves Made*. New York: Vintage, 1972. A detailed and thorough account of slavery as it existed in the plantation South. A rich source of quotes from slaves, slaveholders, and visitors to southern plantations.

James Oliver Horton and Lois E. Horton, *Hard Road to Freedom: The Story of African America*. New Brunswick, NJ: Rutgers University Press, 2001. A general history of blacks in the United States from colonial times.

Nathan Irvin Huggins, *Black Odyssey: The Afro-American Ordeal in Slavery*. New York: Vintage, 1977. A thoughtful description of slavery and its impact on African Americans.

Charles Johnson and Patricia Smith, *Africans in America: America's Journey Through Slavery*. New York: Harcourt Brace, 1998. Provides an informative general history of slavery in the United States; a companion piece to a television presentation with the same name.

Robin D.G. Kelley and Earl Lewis, eds., *To Make Our World Anew: A History of African Americans*. New York: Oxford University Press, 2000. Ten informative chapters following the course of African American history, arranged chronologically. Each chapter is written by a different scholar with a particular interest in the time period.

Alan Lomax, *Folk Songs of North America*. Garden City, NY: Doubleday, 1960. Songs and commentary by one of America's most famous collectors and analysts of traditional music. Includes many examples of slave songs.

John A. Lomax and Alan Lomax, *Best Loved American Folk Songs*. New York: Grosset and Dunlap, 1947. Another volume of folk music and commentary, featuring other songs from the African American tradition.

Henry Mayer, *All on Fire: William Lloyd Garrison and the Abolition of Slavery*. New York: St. Martin's, 1998. A long and thoroughly researched biography of Garrison; full of information about the debate over slavery.

Eric McKitrick, ed., *Slavery Defended: The Views of the Old South*. Englewood Cliffs, NJ: Prentice-Hall, 1963. A collection of primary sources that give the southern perspective on slavery.

August Meier and Elliott Rudwick, eds., *The Making of Black America*. Vol. 1. New York: Atheneum, 1969. Readings on African American history through Reconstruction, covering a wide assortment of topics.

Allan Nevins and Henry Steele Commager, *A Pocket History of the United States*. 6th ed. New York: Pocket, 1976. A good basic history of the United States; provides an overview of the important trends and events, including a solid summary of the effects of slavery on the Union.

Russel B. Nye, *William Lloyd Garrison and the Humanitarian Reformers*.

Boston: Little, Brown, 1955. A short biographical account of Garrison's life and work, with an emphasis on his place within the larger abolitionist movement.

Gilbert Osofsky, ed., *Puttin' On Ole Massa*. New York: Harper and Row, 1969. Three narratives about slavery written by former slaves, or ghostwritten for them by other authors. Useful background commentary is included.

Timothy Severin, *The African Adventure*. New York: Dutton, 1973. The early connections between Africans and Europeans, including information on the rise of the slave trade.

Kenneth Stampp, *The Peculiar Institution*. New York: Knopf, 1967. One of the most influential books ever published on American slavery, and still valuable several decades after its writing. Stampp explores the effect of the institution on slaves, masters, and the life of the South.

Harvey Wish, ed., *Slavery in the South*. New York: Noonday, 1964. A collection of documents about slavery, including writings of former slaves, white slaveholders, and visitors to the South from the North and from abroad.

Donald R. Wright, *African Americans in the Colonial Era*. Arlington Heights, IL: Harlan Davidson, 1990. Discusses the slave trade, the development of slavery in the colonies, and the beginnings of a distinctive black culture in the United States.

Web Sites

Avalon Project at Yale Law School, *Documents on Slavery* (www.yale.edu/lawweb/avalon/slavery.htm). A collection of statutes, eyewitness accounts, recollections, and other documents pertaining to slavery. Includes the Emancipation Proclamation, autobiographical writings of Frederick Douglass, and other important works.

Jerome S. Handler and Michael L. Tuite Jr., *The Atlantic Slave Trade and Slave Life in the Americas: A Visual Record* (http://hitchcock.itc.virginia. edu/Slavery). An intriguing collection of photographs, drawings, and other visual items pertaining to slavery and the slave trade, with brief commentary.

Library of Congress, *Born in Slavery: Slave Narratives from the Federal Writers' Project, 1936–1938* (http://memory.loc.gov/ammem/snhtml/snhome.html). Information and documents relating to the slave narratives collected during the Great Depression.

National Geographic Online, *The Underground Railroad* (www.nationalgeographic.com/railroad/index.html). A site with information about slavery, abolition, and the experiences of fugitive slaves.

WGBH Educational Foundation, *Africans in America* (www.pbs.org/wgbh/aia/home.html). Extensive information about slavery and the African American experience. Based on a PBS television series.

Index

Picture Credits

Cover © CORBIS
© Scala/Art Resource, N.Y., 30–31
© Bettman/CORBIS, 38, 70, 79, 82 (bottom), 87
© Stapleton Collection/CORBIS, 67
© CORBIS, 12, 33, 44 (right), 55
Library of Congress, 8, 20 (both), 27, 47, 49, 82 (right and left), 94, 97, 98
Mary Evans Picture Library, 73
North Wind Picture Archives, 11, 15, 18–19, 36, 41, 42, 44 (left), 52, 58, 63, 69, 74

About the Author

Stephen Currie is the author of more than forty books, including a number of works on history and some historical fiction. Among his books for Lucent are *Life in a Wild West Show*, *The Olympic Games*, and *Adoption*. He is also a teacher. He grew up in Illinois and now lives with his family in upstate New York.